31 Days Toward Passionate

FAITH

31 DAYS TOWARD

Passionate

FAITH

JONI EARECKSON TADA

Multnomah Books

31 DAYS TOWARD PASSIONATE FAITH
published by Multnomah Books

© 2006 by Joni Eareckson Tada
International Standard Book Number: 978-1-60142-550-8

Cover design by James Hall
Cover art/photo by photos.com

Unless otherwise indicated, Scripture quotations are from:
The Holy Bible, New International Version © 1973, 1984 by International Bible Society,
used by permission of Zondervan Publishing House
Other Scripture quotations are from:
The Living Bible (TLB)
© 1971. Used by permission of Tyndale House Publishers, Inc.
All rights reserved.
The Good News Bible: The Bible in Today's English Version (TEV) © 1976 by American Bible Society
New American Standard Bible (NASB) © 1960, 1977 by the Lockman Foundation
The Holy Bible, King James Version (KJV)
The New Testament in Modern English, Revised Edition (Phillips) © 1958, 1960, 1972 by J. B. Phillips

Published in the United States by WaterBrook Multnomah, an imprint of the Crown
Publishing Group, a division of Random House Inc., New York.

MULTNOMAH and its mountain colophon are registered trademarks of Random House Inc.

For information:
Multnomah Books • 12265 Oracle Boulevard, Suite 200 • Colorado Springs, CO 80921

Library of Congress Cataloging-in-Publication Data
Tada, Joni Eareckson.
  31 days toward passionate faith / by Joni Eareckson Tada.
    p. cm.
  ISBN 1-59052-423-3
  1. Christian life—Meditations. 2. Devotional calendars. I. Title.
II. Title: Thirty-one days toward passionate faith.
BV4832.3.T35 2007
242—dc22
                                        2006039114

13 14 15—10 9 8 7 6 5 4 3 2 1

To Daniel Stratman.

May your confidence in Jesus keep growing…and may your faith in Him always be passionate!

Contents

Introduction

OUT OF THE SHALLOWS

There's a river that flows past our old farm back in Maryland, the Patapsco. It meanders past fields and woods, parallels a railroad track, and eventually empties into the Chesapeake Bay.

As a little girl, I used to relish lazy, hazy summer afternoons on the banks of the Patapsco. While my sisters swam, I would wade and splash in the shallows, the cuffs of my pants rolled up past my ankles.

Not once did I venture out into the deep, unknown parts of the river. After all, I was awfully little—and that river was very big.

Yet I envied my sisters who were big enough to dive into the deep parts—places where they could swim and not even touch bottom. To me, my sisters seemed incredibly privileged.

How about you? Are you the sort of person who plays it safe, content with just getting your ankles wet? Or are you the adventurous sort who prefers to get in over your head?

I like to think of this Christian journey of ours as a river. A river of life. As I see it, the shallow places are the common habitat for all believers—the kind of faith and joy and hope we all take part in.

But there is a deeper realm of conscious union with Christ which is far from commonplace. It's the bottomless reservoir we enter only when we begin to exercise a passionate faith.

All believers see Christ, but not all put their fingers into the prints of His nails. Not all put their hand in His wounded side.

Not everyone has the high privilege of John to lean upon Jesus…nor of Paul, to be caught up into a third heaven. It is rare to find believers who live with such sheer abandon for Christ that they leave the shallow places behind and dive into the free-flowing current.

"Most Christians are only up to their ankles in the river of life," wrote Spurgeon. "But few find life a river to swim in, the bottom of which they cannot touch."

It's a risky, wonderful place to be—out in those dark, inscrutable regions where you can't touch bottom no matter how deep you dive. God invites us away from the safety of the bank, away from the measured security of the wading pools where the Christian life is almost easy.

He invites us to a passionate faith. Passion launches us into the adventure. Faith causes us to cling to God for the ride of our lives.

Won't you dive recklessly with me into the depths of Christ through the chapters that follow? Won't you take this voyage? It promises to be, at times, exhilarating. At times heartrendingly painful. For parts of the journey, you'll skim along as though riding on a dolphin's back.

<u>And if your journey is anything like mine, you'll some-
times wonder if you're in danger of drowning.</u>

But whatever your journey holds, if you're continually
immersed in God, and if you progress steadily down the
deepening, broadening river, eventually into the immense
ocean of His eternal presence, you'll be safe. And it will be
worth everything.

Yield yourself up to the strong, sure currents of God's
will and His love. Swim in the depths of His character.

Live passionately, faithfully. In Him.

You and I may begin in the shallows. But if we take
God at His invitation, we dive deeper. Where we stop, no
one has yet discovered...for there, in the awful and mysterious depths of God, there is neither limit nor border nor
end.

CAN'T SAY ENOUGH...

When I was working on my third book, *Choices...Changes*, there was one episode I especially enjoyed writing.

You guessed it. It was the last episode, about my husband.

It was great fun to sit at the computer with my friend and describe Ken Tada. How he looked the first time I saw him...how he talked...how he smiled...how he carried himself...how he moved when he played racquetball. The words about our dating days flowed effortlessly.

Writing about our wedding day and marriage was pure joy. Obviously, I didn't need a thesaurus to think of adjectives. I wanted to go on and on.

And sometimes I did! My friend would have to say, "Uh, Joni, don't you think you've talked enough about Ken's muscles?" Or, "Joni, that's the fourth time in this chapter you've told us how handsome Ken is."

Isn't that funny? I just couldn't say enough good stuff about my husband.

I'll bet it's the same with those you love, too. You want others to know how special that person is—whether it's your mate, your friend, your child, your niece, your nephew, or your grandchild. The best part is finding someone genuinely interested in *listening* to your glowing descriptions. It actually multiplies your pleasure.

Listen in as the author of Hebrews talks about his best Friend, Jesus. It's as if someone approached him and said, "You seem to put a great deal of stock in this Person, Jesus Christ. Just who is He, anyway? Why are you so excited about Him? Can you describe Him?"

Could he ever! Having found a listening ear, the writer can't say enough. Just look at the seven descriptive phrases he uses in the first four verses of his book.

Jumping right in, the writer tells us Jesus is the "appointed heir of all things" (v. 2). Right off the top he lifts Jesus to where He belongs—over all things.

But that's only the beginning. Next the writer reminds us that through the spoken word of Jesus, "he made the universe" (v. 2).

Warming to his subject, the author declares Jesus the very "radiance of God's glory" (v. 3). Just as the brilliance of the sun cannot be separated from the sun itself, Jesus cannot be separated from the glory of the Father—He is God Himself.

Not only does Jesus share in the glory of God, He is "the exact representation of his being" (v. 3). Like a stamp that leaves its impression on warm wax, Jesus is the exact representation of the character and nature of God.

The writer can't stop. Superlatives keep pouring from his pen. He affirms that this mighty Son of God is "sustaining all things by his powerful word" (v. 3). He created the world by the word of His mouth, and now He holds it all together.

But Jesus Christ is more than some awesome, distant Deity, the writer hastens to add. He took notice of our helpless plight and became our Savior. He "provided purification for sins" through the sacrifice of His life on the cross (v. 3). By His death, Christ paid the incalculable penalty for our sins and satisfied every just demand of a holy God.

His work of redemption complete, Jesus "sat down at the right hand of the Majesty in heaven" (v. 3).

With the ink flowing fast on his parchment, the writer goes on and on. Chapter 1, chapter 2, chapter 3, chapter 4...*Jesus, Jesus, Jesus, Jesus.*

How is it with you? Are you looking for listening ears, anxious to go on and on about the Lord Jesus and what He means to you?

If you find you don't have enough adjectives to describe Him, I'd like to introduce you to the author of Hebrews. Sorry I can't give you his name; he got so excited about his Subject he forgot to introduce himself. Maybe the two of you can get away together for a few minutes today.

There's nothing that excited writer would love more than a listening ear.

The Glorious Pursuit

Christ's love compels us, because we are convinced that one died for all, and therefore all died.
And he died for all, that those who live should no
longer live for themselves but for him who died for
them and was raised again…. We are therefore
Christ's ambassadors.

2 CORINTHIANS 5:14–15, 20

Jesus is the reason for everything—not just everything in our
lives, but everything in the universe and throughout all of history.
Of all persons and topics, He is the one most worthy of our words.
Share a few of those life-giving words with someone else. And keep
coming back to the writers of Scripture. They long to tell you more,
so you can know Him better. So you can sound His praises still
more, and more, and more…

THE DISTRACTION DIET

A friend of mine had a baby recently. When I visited the couple's home, I had to admire their elaborate nursery.

They really did it up right! Big Bird nested in the corner, Snuffleupagus perched on the cribside table, and an assortment of wobbling Weebles, Smurfs, and My Little Ponies encircled the interior of the crib. Not to mention five teddy bears. And a busy box gizmo with umpteen handles, knobs, and twirly things. And two musical mobiles. And who knows how many rattles.

This baby was decked out. There was no way this kid was going to get bored or cranky, right?

Well, not exactly. True, the child will be able to amuse himself, what with so many gaudy toys and wild, wonderful distractions. He should find himself positively absorbed at times by the ministrations of the musical mobiles.

The thing is, amusement of that sort lasts for only so long. A child is easily quieted, *so long as he isn't hungry....* But watch out! Once that baby feels the cravings of nature within, absolutely nothing will satisfy but *food!*

So it is with our soul. Distractions and amusements may appease us for a while—church music, candles, processions, banners, committees, and Christian talk shows. But all these, like gaudy toys, will occupy and entertain for only so long. Sooner or later boredom and frustration set in. Once a believer's passion for God is awakened, all of those religious trappings and incidentals simply won't satisfy. Like the writer said in Hebrews 5, you begin to want solid food.

A man or woman animated by the Spirit just *has* to be fed. The cravings of our new nature force us back to the basics—and there begins the glorious pursuit of God. A real Christian will not rest contented with mere appearances. They'll seem like a waste of time.

Are you bored? Restless? Do you refuse to be entertained? Want something more? Are you gathering more spiritual things around you and enjoying them less?

It may be that you're hungry! The cravings of your new nature are giving you hunger pains. And you will not be satisfied until you have real food. Like Jesus says in John 6:35, "I am the bread of life. He who comes to me will never go hungry."

Want to quiet those cravings? Forget the gizmos and doodads in the nursery. The King waits at the dining table.

The Glorious Pursuit

The lions may grow weak and hungry, but those who seek the LORD lack no good thing.

PSALM 34:10

Blessed are those who hunger and thirst for righteousness, for they will be filled.

MATTHEW 5:6

Don't feel hungry at the moment? Maybe you've tuned out that deep inner longing. Maybe you need to reawaken your spiritual taste buds, to accept King David's invitation: "Taste and see that the LORD is good" (Psalm 34:8). Pull up to the table. Open your Bible and see God's heart. Tell your Father a burdensome secret; soak up His forgiveness. Once you've sampled Him, you'll never again be satisfied with junk food.

Day 3

CATCHING UP WITH OUR HEART

Some people find it difficult to think realistically about heaven.

Even Christians feel awkward working toward "eternity," simply because, well…it seems so far away, almost unreal. Something between a Sunday school paper sketch and a half-remembered dream. Even when we try to imagine what it will be like, we come up short of a real desire to go there. Heaven is supposed to be a *place*, not simply a state of mind, but try as we may, it's tough to picture it.

It's little wonder we feel so blasé about it all. The image most people concoct about heaven is anything but appealing. Some imagine it a spooky kind of twilight zone. Others visualize it tucked behind a galaxy where birds chirp and organs play with heavy tremolo and angels bounce from cloud to cloud.

If *that* were a true picture of heaven, I'd be lukewarm about going there, too.

But the fact is that we believers are headed for heaven. It's reality. Heaven may be as near as next year— or next week. So it makes good sense to spend some time here on earth thinking candid thoughts about that future reserved for us.

I admit, it's tough to muster excitement about a place we've never seen. So how do we go about bringing heaven into focus?

Someone once said that Christ brings the heart to heaven first—and then He brings the person. I like that. God knows you and I would have a tough time fixing our eyes on heaven unless our heart was really involved.

That's why our Lord's words in Matthew 6:21 ring so true: "Where your treasure is, there will your heart be also" (KJV).

In other words, if our investments are in heaven, God knows our heart's desire will be there, too.

I'm convinced this little verse in Matthew 6 holds the secret. The only way we can enjoy the thought of heaven, the only way we can start thinking of it as reality, is to allow God to take our heart home first. Once we start investing in eternity, heaven will begin to come into focus. As we give sacrificially of our energies or money, as we spend more time in prayer, praising God and not just petitioning Him, as we witness boldly and fearlessly…we're making deposits in eternity. We're putting more and more of *ourselves* on the other side. As we continue to do these things, we'll wake up one morning to find our heart precisely where it should be…in heaven.

Our future Home won't seem like an eerie twilight zone. It won't fill our thoughts with saccharine visions of bluebirds, chubby angels, and rainbows. No, it will take shape in our minds as the *Real* Estate it actually is, the place where God dwells and prepares for our coming.

"Your eyes will see the king in his beauty and view a land that stretches afar" (Isaiah 33:17). All the other trappings—golden streets, pearly gates, and crystal rivers—aren't nearly as important.

What *is* important is that we will see our King and live with Him forever. In that shining moment we will finally catch up with our hearts—and our heart's desire.

God Himself.

And that will be enough.

The Glorious Pursuit

We fix our eyes not on what is seen, but on what is unseen. For what is seen is temporary, but what is unseen is eternal.

2 CORINTHIANS 4:18

I go to prepare a place for you. If I go and prepare
a place for you, I will come again and receive you
to Myself, that where I am, there you may be also.

JOHN 14:2–3, NASB

*Growing spiritually involves a gradual transfer of our inner
investments from earth to heaven. What portion of your affections
remain down here? How much of your heart have you deposited in
heaven? Take a few moments with your divine Investment Adviser,
and invite Him to help you entrust a little more of yourself to Him.*

Day 4

THE MYTHICAL
STANDSTILL CHRISTIAN

Open up that great book of imaginary beings and leaf through the listings. Somewhere after Centaur, Goblin, E.T., and Mermaid—but before Unicorn or Whatsit—there's a page devoted to an unlikely creature called the Standstill Christian.

It's unlikely because it doesn't exist. There ain't no such thing.

Christians are either growing in the Lord or going backward. That doesn't leave much room in between. It's like true love: It either grows or it begins to die. Love simply can't stand still, and neither can our walk with Christ.

Little wonder the Bible makes growth such a critical issue. Again and again the writers of the New Testament implore believers to keep moving higher, wider, deeper, and stronger. Listen to a few of them. Can you sense the urgency?

> I keep asking that the God of our Lord Jesus
> Christ, the glorious Father, may give you the Spirit
> of wisdom and revelation, so that you may know
> him better.
>
> EPHESIANS 1:17

> And this is my prayer: that your love may abound
> more and more in knowledge and depth of
> insight.
>
> PHILIPPIANS 1:9

One thing I do: Forgetting what is behind and straining toward what is ahead, I press on toward the goal.

PHILIPPIANS 3:13–14

This gospel is bearing fruit and growing, just as it has been doing among you since the day you heard it.

COLOSSIANS 1:6

We pray this in order that you may live a life worthy of the Lord...bearing fruit in every good work, growing in the knowledge of God.

COLOSSIANS 1:10

May the Lord make your love increase and overflow for each other and for everyone else.

1 THESSALONIANS 3:12

You do love all the brothers.... Yet we urge you, brothers, to do so more and more.

1 THESSALONIANS 4:10

We ought always to thank God for you...because
your faith is growing more and more, and the love
every one of you has for each other is increasing.

2 Thessalonians 1:3

Fan into flame the gift of God, which is in you.

2 Timothy 1:6

Let us leave the elementary teachings about Christ
and go on to maturity.

Hebrews 6:1

Like newborn babies, crave pure spiritual milk, so
that by it you may grow up in your salvation.

1 Peter 2:2

But grow in the grace and knowledge of our Lord
and Savior Jesus Christ.

2 Peter 3:18

It goes on and on. There is simply no room for passivity in the Christian faith. Life in Christ is one long string

of action verbs: GROW... PRAISE... LOVE...
LEARN... STRETCH... REACH... PUT OFF... PUT
ON... PRESS ON... FOLLOW... HOLD...
CLEAVE... RUN... WEEP... PRODUCE...
STAND... FIGHT.

In a child, an animal, a flower, or a tree, lack of
growth signals a problem. A healthy life will always show
itself by progress and increase. Anything else begins to
look like death.

So how can you tell if you're growing? Ask yourself a
few simple, direct questions.

Is my sense of sin becoming deeper?

Is my hope brighter?

Is my love more extensive?

Is my spiritual discernment more clear?

Is my faith stronger?

Do I love the Lord Jesus more?

If you can say a hearty yes to these questions, then
you are on the growing side. If not, then you're doing
worse than standing still...you are moving backward.

To put it another way, the Christian's transmission is

equipped with only two gears: Drive and Reverse. There's no such thing as Neutral—let alone Park.

So wake up! There are grave things at stake here. Look—if your foot had gangrene, you would submit to a severe operation, possibly even amputation, to save your life. Your spiritual state is no less grave.

Don't put yourself in that book of strange, imaginary creatures. If you think you're a Standstill Christian, you're only playing a dangerous game of make-believe.

The Glorious Pursuit

I have set before you life and death, blessings and curses. Now choose life.

DEUTERONOMY 30:19

He who is not with me is against me, and he who does not gather with me, scatters.

LUKE 11:23

Day 4

    Growing organisms need a conducive environment and the right diet. In addition, those in the animal kingdom need a third component: exercise. Are you involved in the environment of a supportive, growth-stimulating church? Do you take in a steady diet of God's Word, through teaching, study groups, private reading? And are you actively exercising your spiritual gifts to touch and change lives around you? Ask the Lord to guide your next step.

Day 5

BACKED INTO CORNERS

*J*esus had a way of exasperating people.

He still does. It takes only a glance through one of the Gospels. Before you know it, you find yourself squirming.

The way Jesus does things—the demands He makes, the example He offers, the way He deals with the status quo in people's hearts—all of it backs you into an uncomfortable corner. What He says about sacrifice, favoritism, bigotry, stewardship, and giving presses your back hard against the bricks. Suddenly, unexpectedly, He's got you thinking—thinking about things you never would have troubled yourself with before you picked up His Word.

In short, you're irritated.

The demands of Jesus always seem to bring crisis into people's lives. He commanded Peter to lower his net, even though He knew Peter had been fishing all night with nary a mackerel to show for it.

He told the rich young ruler to sell all his possessions.

He insisted John baptize Him when doing so would violate John's understanding of Messiah.

He demanded that the religious lawyer—who was far more interested in debate and discussion—*do* what he understood rather than simply talking about it.

Uncomfortable corners. Pinned against a spiritual wall.

But the thing I love most about the Lord Jesus is that He won't allow us to stay pinned against the wall. He doesn't want us to remain in our corners. Ah, but the only way He permits us to peel ourselves off those spiritual walls—the only way He allows us to tiptoe out of those uncomfortable corners—is the way of faith: to follow Him.

Jesus will not liberate us from the quandary He's put us in except to have us follow Him and His example. Jesus doesn't assume we will follow Him—it's too precious a thing to leave to us alone. No, He *commands* that we follow Him.

Is He asking something uncomfortable of you today? To clean up a bad habit? To back off your prejudices? To eat some of your pride? To reach deep in your pocket and give to a person in need? To make amends with an irritating friend?

Welcome to the corner! You're in wonderful company! Everyone clashes with the Lord Jesus sooner or later, whether they love Him or hate Him. He exasperates. He engineers crises. He compels. He forces you to make a choice.

Wait long enough in that corner and you'll meet up with Him. But I'm not staying. I'm going to follow Him out.

The Glorious Pursuit

Then [Jesus] said to them all: "If anyone would
come after me, he must deny himself and take up
his cross daily and follow me…. Anyone who does
not carry his cross and follow me cannot be my
disciple."

LUKE 9:23; 14:27

*When Jesus narrows your choices to an uncomfortable few —
or one — it's because He knows any other direction you might go
would be to your loss…and His. Are you feeling "trapped" by the
convicting guidance of His Word? Talk to Him about it now. He
wants to hear about your fears, your guilt, your anger — most of
all, if it involves disobedience, He wants to hear genuine contrition
and see true repentance. Take His hand, and let Him lead you
toward life abundant. Sometimes passionate faith depends more on
the faith part than the passion.*

Day 6

BETWEEN TWO CROSSES

In my weaker moments, I've wondered if the Lord's disciples had as tough a time believing as we do.

After all, they had the benefit of rubbing shoulders with the Master every day for almost three years. As John wrote, Christianity for them was something "which we have heard, which we have seen with our eyes, which we have looked at and our hands have touched" (1 John 1:1).

They were eyewitnesses to the Lord's greatest miracles. They saw dead men raised with a word, lepers healed

with a touch, paralytics leap to their feet at His bidding.
They watched His hands form fresh bread and charcoal-
broiled fish out of thin air—enough to feed thousands of
hungry people. They witnessed a boiling sea and a
screaming wind fall silent and calm in an instant at His
three-word command.

When it comes to the issue of faith, I have to admit,
the disciples aren't the ones I identify with most. But there
is somebody in Scripture who believed in a most extraordinary way.

> One of the criminals who hung there hurled
> insults at [Jesus]: "Aren't you the Christ? Save
> yourself and us!"
>
> But the other criminal rebuked him. "Don't
> you fear God," he said, "since you are under the
> same sentence? We are punished justly, for we are
> getting what our deeds deserve. But this man has
> done nothing wrong."
>
> Then he said, "Jesus, remember me when you
> come into your kingdom."

Jesus answered him, "I tell you the truth,
today you will be with me in paradise."

LUKE 23:39–43

Yes, it was marvelous for the disciples to believe in
Jesus. With the exception of the betrayer, those men stuck
with the Lord through golden days of glory and storm-
darkened days of anxiety and gloom. They had left
everything to follow the Lord—even at the risk of their
very lives.

But to me, it was an even greater display of faith for
this dying felon to put his trust in the Lord. That man on
the adjacent cross never had the benefit of seeing all the
mighty signs and miracles which flabbergasted the disciples. He never shared in their quiet talks around the
evening campfires. He never enjoyed their camaraderie
under full sail in an open boat under a wide Galilean sky.

The criminal saw only Jesus in agony, in suffering,
and in weakness. He saw Him deserted, mocked, naked,
humiliated, and despised. He witnessed no majesty and
power—*and yet he believed*.

But whatever this story says about the faith of a penitent thief, it says even more about the One who responded.

The Lord Jesus never gave so complete a proof of His power and will to save as He did upon that occasion. In the day when He seemed most weak, He showed that He was a strong deliverer. In the hour when the Lord's body was racked with pain, He showed that He could feel tenderly for others. At the time when He Himself was dying, He conferred on a wicked criminal eternal life.

If there was ever a time when Jesus deserved to think a little about His own comfort, it was on the cross. But even there, His thoughts were of others. He offered them hope; He offered them life.

He was reaching out to redeem.

The encounter between those two crosses on that dark day is a story of unceasing wonder. That the same dying Savior would reach down the centuries to save you and me is more wonderful still.

The Glorious Pursuit

Thomas said to him, "My Lord and my God!"
Then Jesus told him, "Because you have
seen me, you have believed; blessed are those
who have not seen and yet have believed."

JOHN 20:28–29

Though you have not seen him, you love him; and
even though you do not see him now, you believe
in him and are filled with an inexpressible and glorious joy, for you are receiving the goal of your
faith, the salvation of your souls.

1 PETER 1:8–9

*Ask your unseen Lord to strengthen your faith in Him and
your love for Him by showing you the many visible evidences of His
presence in your life.*

QUALITY AND QUANTITY

*H*ave you ever wondered why Jesus launched His public ministry by turning water into wine at a wedding party?

Just last night I puzzled over that question as I read the second chapter of John. Why that particular miracle at that particular time? And why wine?

I once heard my friend, Bible teacher Kay Arthur, describe that miracle as one of the highest *quality and quantity.* "That," she exclaimed, "is the way Jesus does things!"

Let's think about that. Those six stone jars Jesus told the servants to fill with water were huge. Each container held up to *thirty gallons*. Have you ever tried to lift or carry thirty gallons of anything? And those servants, Scripture tells us, filled each jar "to the brim." It must have been tough hauling those enormous jugs from the well into the house.

When Jesus changed that plain Galilean water into Chablis (or whatever it was) the wedding party ended up with 180 gallons of it! That, my friends, is a lot of wine. There's no way folks at the wedding would be able to drink that much, that fast. It was far more than they needed. Surely, one thirty-gallon jar would have been plenty. Hadn't the guests already consumed every drop of wine in the house?

But Jesus chose to provide in quantity. He gave much more than anyone would have expected.

And then there was the quality of that wine. This wasn't "California Cooler." It wasn't plain-label jug stuff. It was strictly gold medallion—probably ten grades above the best contemporary French vintage. The quality of that miraculous wine was absolute tops.

The master of the banquet was incredulous after he tasted the fresh supply. "Why in the world did you save the best for last?" he asked the bridegroom. "You could have gotten by with a bargain brand at this point in the feast!"

But Jesus chose to provide with quality. He gave much better than anyone would have expected.

It was as Kay Arthur said: a miracle of quality and quantity. And that's what He wants to do in your life today. He says to you as He said to His disciples long ago: "I have come that [you] may have life, and have it to the full" (John 10:10). The life He's talking about, of course, is *His* life, flowing in and through you.

When it comes to *quantity*, this is life that bubbles up and spills over the rim. More than you ever expected or could possibly contain.

When it comes to *quality*, this is the very life of God. We can, as Peter says, "participate in the divine nature" (2 Peter 1:4). It is the best life that can be.

The key? Well, let's give some credit to Mary, the Lord's mother. The counsel she gave to those servants that day at the wedding can hardly be improved upon: "Do whatever he tells you" (John 2:5).

Submit to His Lordship with passionately obedient faith. Do exactly as He says…and be prepared for a life full of surprises.

The Glorious Pursuit

I tell you the truth, anyone who has faith in me [Jesus] will do what I have been doing. He will do even greater things than these, because I am going to the Father.

JOHN 14:12

Give, and it will be given to you. A good measure, pressed down, shaken together and running over, will be poured into your lap.

LUKE 6:38

Day 7

The riches God wishes to pour out into our lives are far beyond our dreams. But His wealth is of a different nature than what the world counts as wealth—His is far better! Ask your Father to broaden your dreams, to encompass more and more of the quality and quantity of life He has for you. And invite Him to change your values, so you'll recognize His abundance when He sends it your way.

THE UNSEEN SOURCE

When I was a child on our family's farm, one of my favorite places was the pond down in the pasture by the barn. It was filled with tadpoles, crayfish, and—oh, all kinds of attractions for an adventurous little girl on a hot summer afternoon.

As a child, I always wondered where the water in the pond came from. I'd walk all the way around its edge but could never see any stream splashing into it. No waterfall. No pipes. What was flowing into the pond to make it so fresh and clear and full?

Day 8

My dad patiently tried to explain that the pond was fed by a spring, a source of water from deep down in the earth. That spring, he told me, bubbled up from within and filled the little pond area.

To me it was a big mystery. But I was satisfied with the answer and went contentedly on my way, playing with the frogs and crayfish.

I don't know how many times that little spring has come to my mind through the years...especially when I think about the Holy Spirit.

Let me explain.

We've all heard people say we should be "filled with the Holy Spirit." Now, that's good, biblical counsel. Ephesians 5:18 says, "Do not get drunk on wine, which leads to debauchery. Instead, be filled with the Spirit."

What kind of image does that create in your mind? How many of us picture the Spirit being poured into our lives from the *outside*...as if we were hollow mannequins?

Just unscrew the cap on top of our heads, Lord, and fill us from the toes on up!

Do we get the idea that God's Spirit is being carried

around in a massive pitcher, ready to be ladled out to us for the asking?

That thought reminds me of my old confusion about the farm pond. I kept looking for some stream pouring in. An outside source. Yet, when the Bible talks about us being filled with the Spirit, it's more accurate to picture a *spring*. When we obey God and yield our lives to Him, emptying ourselves of selfish desires, the Spirit of God is just like a spring bubbling up within us…from down deep in our souls. The Spirit source fills us and we are satisfied.

As Jesus said: "'He who believes in Me, as the Scripture said, "From His innermost being will flow rivers of living water."' But this He spoke of the Spirit, whom those who believed in Him were to receive" (John 7:38–39, NASB).

If my dad would have dug out a larger pond area in the dirt, that little spring would have continued to fill it. That might be good advice for you and me. If we would empty ourselves even further, letting go of our own rights, clearing out the debris of habitual sins, and humbling ourselves further before the Lord, our *capacity* for God's Spirit would be increased.

He would fill us even more.

As our lives brim over from this ever-fresh wellspring within us, there will be plenty of refreshment for the thirsty souls of those around us.

The Glorious Pursuit

The wind blows wherever it pleases. You hear its sound, but you cannot tell where it comes from or where it is going. So it is with everyone born of the Spirit.

JOHN 3:8

I will sprinkle clean water on you, and you will be clean; I will cleanse you from all your impurities and from all your idols. I will give you a new heart and put a new spirit in you; I will remove from you your heart of stone and give you a heart of flesh. And I will put my Spirit in you and move

you to follow my decrees and be careful to keep
my laws.

EZEKIEL 36:25—27

*When you're overflowing with the Holy Spirit's life, you will
see the evidence in your thoughts, words, and actions—they will all
reflect the holiness of God. And a life that reflects God's purity
can't help but have an impact on others around you. What evidence
do you see of the Spirit's upwelling inside you? How can you clear
sinful obstructions from the flow or expand your capacity for His
abundant life?*

IGNORING THE ODDS

*Y*ou've had it happen to you. You're in a tough situation, you pray about it, and the Spirit of God answers—but *not* in the way you'd expect. You find the Lord Jesus asking you to handle your tough situation in a way you would have never anticipated! Let's say it's a problem in the office. After much prayer, you sense the Spirit of God urging you to talk to your supervisor.

No way, Lord! you say to Him. *If I bring these things up before my boss, my job security goes down the drain!*

But despite your protests, the Spirit of Christ keeps pushing you the way of passionate faith, prompting you to handle that tough situation *His* way—not in the manner you would normally choose.

Isn't that just like the Lord? *We* think God should have us manage a sticky job situation or domestic tangle one way. The "obvious" way. The "logical" way. After all, handling the matter with simple common sense improves your odds that everything will turn out right...right?

Wrong! God often calls us to ignore the odds, asking us to face our problems His way. And His way is sometimes most unorthodox.

Have you ever taken time to consider General Joshua's dilemma, described in Joshua 6? The Lord met with Joshua prior to the battle of Jericho, identifying Himself as "the commander of the army of the LORD" (Joshua 5:14).

What a relief, Joshua may have thought. *Now the Lord will lay out an infallible battle plan for attacking that powerful, walled city.*

Day 9

Well, Joshua got his battle plan, all right. But it certainly couldn't have been what he was expecting. Talk about an irrational, unorthodox way of handling a problem! Think about it: The Lord wanted Joshua and his army to march around Jericho for six days without saying a word. Then on the seventh day they were to make the circuit seven times, listen for a trumpet blast, and then yell real loud!

Now I ask you, does that sound like common sense?

The book of Joshua, however, records that the Israelites followed God's instructions to a T. In spite of the risks, in the face of ridiculous odds, they simply did as the Lord had said. The result was one of the most dazzling victories in Israel's long history.

What is God asking you to do today that seems a little...unorthodox? Has the Commander of the Lord's army presented you with a highly unusual battle plan?

Ignore the odds and obey.

In the long run, you can't lose.

The Glorious Pursuit

"My thoughts are not your thoughts, neither are your ways my ways," declares the LORD. "As the heavens are higher than the earth, so are my ways higher than your ways and my thoughts than your thoughts."

ISAIAH 55:8–9

The foolishness of God is wiser than man's wisdom, and the weakness of God is stronger than man's strength.

1 CORINTHIANS 1:25

What risk of obedience is the Lord placing before you at this moment? What are you trying not to hear Him saying? What might you lose if you listen? What victory might He win if you obey? Ask Him for courageous wisdom—His wisdom—to take this step of passionate faith.

STILL LIFE?

As an artist, I've always been challenged by still life. Contrary to what you might think, still life has to be more than a collection of objects occupying space on a table. Those images must compel the viewer to become involved. They must unlock memories, evoke mental images. While the painting itself doesn't move, it must move something within one who views it.

No, a bowl of fruit doesn't jump around, but it *does* have life. The challenge is to make a banana look like it's begging to be peeled. Dying to get eaten.

When I paint a bell, I want that bell to do what it was made to do. A painted bell that doesn't *ring* in the viewer's mind is a dead thing. Something less than a bell.

If I paint a candle, I want the viewer to smell the fragrance of melting wax and feel the heat of the flame.

Fruit. Bells. Candles. These must be more than lifeless ornaments. They must perform their appointed tasks in the imagination of the one who stands before the painting. Why? Because that is what we expect of their real-life counterparts. A piece of fruit that sits undisturbed and uneaten in a bowl will soon rot—unless it's made of wax. An ornamental candle that languishes for years in a brass holder never fulfills its destiny. A voiceless bell that collects dust on somebody's knickknack shelf is a mockery to its creator.

As I consider these thoughts, it comes to me that some of us Christians have become "still life." We give every appearance of pious, churchgoing, Bible-believing disciples of Jesus. But we're still life—and we know it. A one-dimensional painting. An ornament on display. A knickknack on the shelf. Nice to look at and be looked up to…but rarely put to good use. Down in our hearts, we know we're gathering dust, letting the years slip by, not really doing and being what God intended us to do and be.

The book of James offers succinct counsel for ornamental Christians. "Do not merely listen to the word, and so deceive yourselves," the apostle writes. *"Do what it says"* (James 1:22, emphasis mine).

Just as bells are meant to ring, you and I are meant to sound out the good news of Jesus.

Just as candles are meant to burn, you and I are meant to stir the fiery, holy passion of the Spirit within us.

Just as fruit is meant to nourish and refresh, you and I are meant to bear the fragrant, life-giving fruit of the Spirit of Christ for the sake of hungry, discouraged men and women.

Life, you see, is never really still.

Only death is still.

The Glorious Pursuit

Woe to him who quarrels with his Maker…. Does
the clay say to the potter, "What are you making?"
Does your work say, "He has no hands"?

ISAIAH 45:9

We are God's workmanship, created in Christ
Jesus to do good works, which God prepared in
advance for us to do.

EPHESIANS 2:10

*You were created for a purpose. You were carefully honed and
crafted in the mind of God in eternity past. You were designed with
a unique set of talents, passions, and values in order to fulfill a
special mission. Now you've been launched into life, and God is
watching eagerly to see the outcome of His workmanship. How's it
going? If you're not certain, take the next small step of obedience,
and see what He does. Remember, the hand of your Maker has
never left you.*

Day 11

HIGHER SERVICE

My husband is the strong, silent type—the picture of a robust, athletic man. As such, he can be an intimidating force on the racquetball court.

Perhaps that's why a few of his racquetball buddies express surprise when they learn Ken is married to a quadriplegic in a wheelchair.

"It's really amazing," they say, "that you've given up your life to serve a handicapped woman."

That sort of comment isn't uncommon. You hear

people talking about the burden of caring for an elderly mother or the sacrifice of serving a sick child or of devoting years to a handicapped youngster. Sometimes people will say a woman has "given her husband the best years of her life" or a missionary couple has given "tireless service" in a foreign country.

Pondering statements like these has led me to a question: *Just whom do we think these people are serving?*

Listen to Paul's words: "Whatever you do, do your work heartily, as for the Lord rather than for men, knowing that from the Lord you will receive the reward of the inheritance. It is the Lord Christ whom you serve" (Colossians 3:23–24, NASB).

Ken has not given his life to serve a handicapped woman. He's given his life to serve Christ. He just happens to be married to someone with a disability.

It's the same with anyone who serves in the Lord's name. How can service to the Lord Christ be a tedious, boring effort—or even a sacrifice? Certainly we tire of our service to men, "causes," organizations, companies, or aca-

demic institutions. No doubt Ken gets very tired of helping me through my nightly routine. I get tired, too. Yet,
however tiring our work may be, how could it ever be *tiresome*? How could it be anything less than a joy to serve the
One who has given us all things for life and enrichment
and enjoyment—Jesus, who suffered so much to secure
our salvation?

Have you ever sensed a lack of purpose in your work?
Have you struggled to see the reward for all your effort?
Is it all getting a little wearisome?

*Why go the extra mile for this company? They'll never reward
me for it.*

*Why put fabric softener on his shirt? He'll never notice any-
way.*

*He never says anything about my new recipes. Why do I keep
trying?*

*Why should I put myself out on this English assignment? It'll
be graded by some graduate assistant anyway. The prof will never
see it.*

Maybe—just maybe—you've been doing your work

for the notice and praise of men. Maybe you've been laboring for your own personal gratification. Talk about tiresome! That kind of service can get very old and stale. Fast.

It's the motive that counts. Doing your work wholeheartedly "as for the Lord" can transform virtually any task you're called on to perform...whether it's counting widgets in a widget factory, writing a term paper in economics, cleaning the kitchen for the umpteenth time, or giving loving care to someone who fails to acknowledge or appreciate you.

The Lord Jesus will neither overlook nor forget the tasks you perform in His name. Nor will He fail to reward you.

"Therefore, my dear brothers, stand firm. Let nothing move you. Always give yourselves fully to the work of the Lord, because you know that your labor in the Lord is not in vain" (1 Corinthians 15:58).

The Glorious Pursuit

If we live, we live to the Lord; and if we die, we die to the Lord. So, whether we live or die, we belong to the Lord.

ROMANS 14:8

Whatever you do, whether in word or deed, do it all in the name of the Lord Jesus, giving thanks to God the Father through him.

COLOSSIANS 3:17

Passion for service to people is a good thing, but it will deflate quickly if it doesn't flow from passion for Christ. Fix Jesus firmly in your mind and heart. Put Him at the top of your "company flowchart." He's your loving Master. When you're serving "the least of these," you're serving Him (see Matthew 25:31–46).

Day 12

LET DOWN YOUR NET

It was one of those dry times.

The Bible seemed about as inspiring as the Los Angeles phone book. Prayer felt like an exercise in futility. My prayers never seemed to make it more than two or three feet into the air. I would have been happy to get them as high as the ceiling.

My Christian friends kept going on and on about all they were learning and how they were growing and what God was telling them and *wasn't the Lord wonderful*? I felt little interest in spiritual things. Faking it made me feel even more guilty.

The hardest part was that I couldn't trace the dry spell to anything specific. No besetting sins. No fights with my husband. No roots of bitterness. No great lapses in my prayer life or Bible study. No lack of fellowship.

Yet my spirit felt as arid as July in the Mojave Desert. It was like those times when your smile loses its shine, your soul becomes dim, and your countenance tells you and everyone around you that something's not quite right.

Strange as it sounds, the closest biblical analogy I can find for those dry days takes place in the middle of a lake. Let's pick up the story in Luke chapter 5.

> [Jesus] got into one of the boats, the one belonging to Simon, and asked him to put out a little from shore. Then he sat down and taught the people from the boat.
>
> When he had finished speaking, he said to Simon, "Put out into deep water, and let down the nets for a catch."

Simon answered, "Master, we've worked hard all night and haven't caught anything. But because you say so, I will let down the nets."

When they had done so, they caught such a large number of fish that their nets began to break. So they signaled their partners in the other boat to come and help them, and they came and filled both boats so full that they began to sink.

When Simon Peter saw this, he fell at Jesus' knees and said, "Go away from me, Lord; I am a sinful man!"

Luke 5:3–8

That's a story for dry times—when you feel a little tired of trying…when you're a little weary of praying prayers that don't seem to get answered…when the pages of the Bible might as well be written in Egyptian hieroglyphics.

Simon, too, was weary. Tired of trying. His back ached and his eyelids drooped. He'd been at it all night long without so much as a sardine to show for it. Yet at the command of Christ, he let down his nets. One more time.

Perhaps all of your nets are empty today. You've tried and tried but come up with nothing. You feel dry and dull, and you wonder if God has misplaced your file somewhere on His desk.

He hasn't! God has been listening to your prayers. As a matter of fact, it's often those petitions offered in the dry times that please Him best.

Your heavy heart is no secret to the God who loves you. As David wrote: "All my longings lie open before you, O Lord; my sighing is not hidden from you" (Psalm 38:9).

He's asking you today to let down your net. One more time. Even though you haven't seen amazing results in recent weeks. Even though your emotions say, "What's the use?" Even though running an uphill marathon seems more appealing than seeking the Lord right now. Nevertheless, obey the word of Christ and let down your net. Keep in the Word. Return to prayer. Confess your sin. Get accountable to a Christian friend. Worship with

God's people. Sooner or later, He'll surprise you just like He surprised Simon Peter. He's going to bring you out of that long night—out of that dryness. You're going to experience His joy…more than you can handle.

Be faithful. Trust Him. Wait.

Jesus can still fill an empty net.

The Glorious Pursuit

He gives strength to the weary and increases the power of the weak. Even youths grow tired and weary, and young men stumble and fall; but those who hope in the LORD will renew their strength. They will soar on wings like eagles; they will run and not grow weary, they will walk and not be faint.

ISAIAH 40:29—31

God has not given up on you. Don't give up on Him. Seek Him now in prayer and in His Word.

Day 13

A TWOFOLD DEFENSE

What's your first response when you're hit with temptation?

An impulse to back away from your testimony…to fudge the truth…to spread a bit of gossip…to dwell on an impure mental image?

In our daily warfare with sin, it is our Enemy's *first approach* that can be the most dangerous. Bolt the door firmly against his first knock, and it will be easier to keep it closed when he begins pounding and kicking later on. At the beginning of His ministry, our Example showed us a powerful way to thwart temptation's first approach. Satan chose his time carefully. After almost six weeks of fasting in the wild wastes of the Sinai, Jesus must have been faint with hunger.

At that moment of profound human weakness, the devil came calling.

The tempter came to him and said, "If you are the Son of God, tell these stones to become bread."

Jesus answered, "It is written: 'Man does not live on bread alone, but on every word that comes from the mouth of God'" (Matthew 4:3–4).

Jesus countered attack after attack by quoting Scripture after Scripture, foiling each satanic strike. In so doing, He sketched a wonderful pattern for us.

But Scripture isn't the only defensive weapon in our God-given arsenal. Consider another example Jesus laid down—not at the beginning of His ministry, but at the end.

In the Garden of Gethsemane, the marshaled forces of hell tore at our Lord's humanity, trying to keep Him from the cross. If we could have somehow observed that scene, it would have been a terrifying moment. Had Jesus turned away from Calvary, you and I would be lost for eternity.

Just as the devil had enticed Jesus three times in the wilderness, so He was tempted three times in the Garden.

But what does Jesus do this time? *He prays.* And although His friends—His disciples—don't even stay awake to encourage Him, He continues to pour out His soul. Groaning. Sweating. Agonizing. Lying facedown. Maybe there's more than one reason that this and the following hours are referred to as His "passion."

At the dawn of His ministry Jesus showed us the importance of using Scripture to fight our Enemy. At sunset, He underscored the use of prayer.

Scripture and prayer—those are the weapons. Well do we know that we should use both. But how hard it is in the middle of our problems to remember these examples of Christ!

Jesus understands even that.

For when He was tempted in the Garden, the Son of Man spoke such human words: "The spirit is willing, but the flesh is weak" (Matthew 26:41, NASB). Jesus knew how strong the pull of temptation could be.

Are you weak today, even though your spirit is willing? Are you tempted to open the door "just for a moment" to that persistent knocking?

Whatever the assault may be, it can be overcome. Jesus showed us how, both at the beginning and at the end of His ministry on earth.

Just another reminder that He's with us from start to finish.

The Glorious Pursuit

No temptation has seized you except what is common to man. And God is faithful; he will not let you be tempted beyond what you can bear. But when you are tempted, he will also provide a way out so that you can stand up under it.

1 CORINTHIANS 10:13

The way out of temptation must always be truth-based. That's why you need to be saturated in God's Word. And the way of escape must always be trust-based, depending utterly on God as our Warrior. That's why you need to live in an attitude of prayer. On what door is the Enemy knocking—or pounding—right now? Run to God. Let Him hold the perimeter, so you can rest safely inside His protective embrace.

Day 14

COMING HOME TO GOD'S WORD

My husband Ken came home from a fishing trip last Saturday afternoon and plopped contentedly into his favorite chair.

"This is great," he sighed. "I've looked forward to coming home."

He'll never know how much that little comment warmed my heart. I so much want our home to be a place of refreshment for him, a place where he likes to spend his time.

I think that's what Paul was talking about when he
told the Colossians, "Let the word of Christ dwell in you
richly" (3:16, KJV). Or, as Phillips translates the verse,
"Let the full richness of Christ's teaching find its home
among you."

God intends His Word to *dwell* within us, to make its
home in us. What a poignant way to put it. Think how
well you know your own home—or perhaps the home
where you grew up. Visualize its rooms and hallways, its
closets and cupboards. You know it like the back of your
hand, don't you?

You know what's in the linen closet.

Where the glass measuring cups are stored.

The squeak of the linoleum tile by the washing
machine.

The way the rafters creak on a cold night.

Which part of the roof leaks when it rains.

Exactly how many minutes somebody can be in the
shower before the hot water runs out.

The way the dining room looks in the moonlight.

The smell of your old cedar chest.

Home. A place of familiarity and relaxation. A place to build memories. The focus for so many of our hopes and longings.

When Paul said, "Let the word of Christ dwell in you richly," he was reminding us that Scripture should find a home in our hearts, that we should live in its light. And we should know it, much like any other home, like the back of our hands. We should be able to place where most things are in its pages. We should go to God's Word because we prefer it—we're familiar with its commands and we relax in its promises.

I can visualize one dear old saint who has lived comfortably in the Word of God for seventy-five years. Not only can he quote chapter after chapter verbatim from his old Bible, he can tell you where individual verses appear on the pages! When it comes to the Bible, this man's at home.

How many of us actually consider God's Word a "dwelling place"? Does it truly *live* in our hearts, or is Scripture something we just kind of visit for occasional refreshment, like a vacation spot?

God wants His Word to be a home to us—a strong refuge, a warm and restful sanctuary from the bumps, bruises, and perplexities of everyday life.

Let His Word live in you with all of its richness, promises, teaching, and direction. Let it be your retreat from a cynical, pressure-filled world. Let it make you rich in true wisdom.

Wherever life takes you, wherever your road leads, home can be as close as your heart.

The Glorious Pursuit

I have hidden your word in my heart that I might not sin against you.

PSALM 119:11

Many people believe that Scripture memorization is something they could never do. Or that they don't have time for it. But both of these assumptions are, happily, false. Choose a short, meaningful verse from Scripture, or part of a verse—any true statement that would change the way you think and live if you were to internalize it. Write it on a card and carry it around with you for the next week. At least three times each day, simply take it out and read it slowly a few times. Think about the meaning of the words and phrases, and the difference it needs to make in your heart and life. Pray about it. Before the week is over, you'll most likely have memorized the words—or at least the verse's significance. This is one way to let God's Word dwell in you richly.

PRAYER APPRECIATION

*H*ave you ever wondered how people can spend thousands of dollars on a *painting,* of all things?

Or how someone can stand for twenty minutes in front of a Rembrandt in a museum? Or how folks can ooh and ahh over a sculpture or an Ansel Adams photograph?

Do you ever scratch your head and wonder just what people see in art?

Or take music. Does it puzzle you that people buy season tickets to the symphony—and hardly miss a performance? Why do people listen for hours to Bach? And what's so captivating about a Mendelssohn concerto or a Strauss waltz or a Chopin minuet?

Oh sure, you admit they all have their fine points. Art and music are nice to occasionally dabble in, but come on—how is it that some people go overboard on such things?

If you feel that way...I understand. I used to shrug my shoulders toward art and music, too. I suppose I was lacking what they call "appreciation."

But I also remember when that ho-hum, scratch-your-head attitude began to change. It all started when my art teacher sat down with me and started flipping through pages and pages of art books. At almost every page, he would stop and linger over a Monet print or a Cézanne reproduction. He would spend hours discussing the composition and color in a painting by Mary Cassatt.

At first I felt...well, bored. But the more I looked and listened, the more I began to appreciate. Spending time with the masters elevated my thinking. I began to see things I had never seen. The more I looked, the more was revealed, and the more I understood.

Now when I see someone stand for long minutes in front of a Rembrandt, I smile and nod my head. I can identify.

If you don't appreciate good art, then go to a museum and start *looking* at good art. If you don't appreciate fine music, go to a concert and *listen* to fine music.

I know people who have a similar struggle when they look at the prayer habits of others. They listen to someone getting all excited about spending a morning talking to the Lord, and can only shake their heads. They will be the first to admit they simply do not appreciate the work of prayer.

Frankly, the only way you and I can develop a real appreciation for prayer is to take a small step of faith and simply…pray. Prayer itself is an art which only the Holy Spirit can teach.

Pray for prayer.

Pray to be helped in prayer.

Pray until you appreciate prayer.

Like art, like music, like so many other disciplines, prayer can only be appreciated when you actually spend time in it. Spending time with the Master will elevate your thinking and strengthen your spiritual passion. The more you pray, the more will be revealed. You will understand. You will smile and nod your head as you identify with others who fight long battles and find great joy on their knees.

You will appreciate not only the greatness of prayer, but the greatness of God.

The Glorious Pursuit

By day the LORD directs his love, at night his song is with me—a prayer to the God of my life.

PSALM 42:8

Then Jesus told his disciples a parable to show them that they should always pray and not give up.

LUKE 18:1

Want to deepen your prayer appreciation—and the passion of your faith? If you're new to the subject of prayer, start with five minutes. Right now. Turn to one of the psalms of praise and recite God's Word back to Him as a prayer. Or pour out whatever is on your heart to God, as you would to a trusted friend. Think back on the blessings of today or the day before and recount them in a litany of gratitude to the Lord. Tell Him what you love about Him. Think of some areas in your life you'd like His help in changing—take a deep breath and confess those things before Him, asking for His Spirit-inspired assistance. Now go on with your day. But set another brief appointment with Him tomorrow. And the next day. And the next...

Day 16

HIGH-ALTITUDE
ATTITUDE

When life rushes by too fast, when deadlines pile up and commitments mount by the hour…I begin longing for the Sierras.

The world seems a little less crazy after a couple of days on top of a mountain. Those high country panoramas have a way of clearing my head and giving me a fresh perspective. The world and its problems seem a little less overwhelming. Pressures seem somehow less pressing. Life begins to look manageable again.

That's why Psalm 61 remains a real favorite for me. I love it when David says, "From the ends of the earth I call to you, I call as my heart grows faint; lead me to the rock that is higher than I. For you have been my refuge, a strong tower against the foe" (vv. 2–3).

God is the rock that is higher than you and I. And when our world presses in on us, when deadlines circle like vultures, when commitments cut into our shoulders like a ninety-pound pack, we need renewed perspective. We need a vantage point.

Spending time with God, in the high places of His power and love, we can gain a better, wider view on our lives. He is the mountain towering over our smoggy horizons. Life viewed from His heights can clear our minds, help us sort through priorities, and allow us to see how our days can be managed after all.

Maybe, like me, you've had one whirlwind of a month. You face demands from your family, frustrations at work, commitments at church, and expectations from friends. You feel your heart growing fainter with each added pressure.

You may not be able to take time off and head for the mountains (especially if you live in Kansas). But you can still climb that Rock so much higher than you.

Investing solid, concentrated time with your understanding Lord will give you a whole new outlook. From the summit of His love, you'll see things as they really are.

The Glorious Pursuit

[Jesus] took Peter, John and James with him and went up onto a mountain to pray.

LUKE 9:28

What life "lenses" are threatening to distort your view of reality? Pressures? Worries? Relational problems? Sin? Time for a vision check. Ask God to help you put it all out of your mind, at least for a few minutes. Ask His pardon, if necessary, for any offense you've committed against Him. Enjoy His forgiveness. Bathe in His peace. Express your repentance. Let Him disburse the fog, wipe away the grime from your windshield. Then ease back into your day, walking a little higher above the world's fray.

Day 17

WHEN GOD STOOD STILL

He felt the excitement before he heard the sound.

Something—someone—was coming down the highway. The noise of a crowd boiling out of the city gates. It was like a wave, about to break over the top of him. He was that close.

"What is it?" he shouted. "What's coming?"

A voice answered him from the darkness—the perpetual, all-encompassing darkness he had always known.

"Jesus of Nazareth is coming this way."

He started yelling. Yelling like there was no tomorrow. Yelling until he thought his throat would split.

"JESUS! Son of David! Have mercy on me!"

A cuff came out of the darkness. A kick. Harsh, grating words.

"Hush, you fool!"

"Shut up!"

"Hold your tongue!"

"Can't someone silence that man?"

He paid them no mind, no mind at all. He only shouted all the more.

"Son of David, have *mercy* on me!"

The Nazarene stood still and ordered the man to be brought to Him. When he came near, Jesus asked him, "What do you want me to do for you?"

I've always loved that portion of Mark chapter 10. There have been many times when I've felt just like Bartimaeus, the blind beggar at the gates of Jericho.

Somehow I've aimlessly wandered off the path God has put me on. I've sinned—maybe deliberately, perhaps thoughtlessly. And I feel so far from God. I picture myself lost in a crowd, pushed to the side of the road, groping in the dark. I want to find my way back to the right path but sometimes feel too ashamed or discouraged to even approach God in prayer.

I foolishly imagine God is busy somewhere else, tending to the prayers of other people who are more sincere, more valuable to the kingdom.

When things get that way, I picture poor Bartimaeus—lost and going nowhere. And sometimes, even though I don't shout, I feel like whispering the words.

Jesus, Son of David, have mercy on me.

And somehow the hustle and bustle of the crowd stops.

The Lord hears the call.

I love those two little words that describe the action that Jesus took.

"And Jesus stood still…" (Mark 10:49, KJV).

The Lord actually stopped what He was doing. The God of the universe stood still and beckoned the poor beggar to be brought to Him…simply because he asked for mercy.

I've wondered why the Lord was so moved by this one man. Surely there were other beggars in the crowd, just as lost, going nowhere. But this man had cried out from his heart. He wanted mercy. And he sincerely believed Jesus could deliver him.

That's what I need to remember when I've wandered away from the path God has put me on…when I've carelessly ignored the truth.

Hebrews 4:16 says that when we approach the throne of grace with confidence, we do so that first we may receive *mercy*. Only after that will we find grace to help us in our time of trouble.

We needn't fear that Jesus is busy elsewhere in His vast universe. Or tending to the prayers of the "super saints." Right now if you sense a deep spiritual need, if you feel the weight of guilt or regret crushing your shoulders, remember that Jesus of Nazareth is passing by.

Call out for mercy. And for you, God will stand still.

The Glorious Pursuit

The LORD, the LORD, the compassionate and gracious God, slow to anger, abounding in love and faithfulness, maintaining love to thousands, and forgiving wickedness, rebellion and sin.

EXODUS 34:6−7

If we confess our sins, he is faithful and just and will forgive us our sins and purify us from all unrighteousness.

1 JOHN 1:9

Crying out for mercy is the easiest thing to do—we just utter the words. And it's the hardest thing to do—we run up against the barrier of our own pride. But when we come to recognize that we are desperately needy and that our pride is the greatest barrier to fellowship with God, then we can let go of all pretense and bow humbly and gratefully before the Almighty. Humility is the complete opposite of pride—and it's the most important foundation stone of a passionate faith.

Day 18

THE LEAKY BUCKET

On the farm when we were kids, my sisters and I got involved in 4-H projects. One of those projects was raising calves. Oh boy, were they cute. I used to love to pet that silky, curly hair between their ears. It felt funny to get a nuzzle with a wet muzzle—and their tongues were like warm, wet sandpaper.

Feeding time was a chore—but we sure laughed a lot. My sister had a milk formula which she had to mix and pour into a bucket—a bucket with a big nipple on the bottom for the calf to suck on.

I remember one time when the only bucket I could find had a little hole in the bottom. The calf was bleating and crying for his dinner and there just wasn't another bucket around. There was no one to hop into the truck, drive to the feed store, and pick up a new one. I looked into the woeful face of that little calf and decided the only thing I could use was the leaky bucket.

First, I made certain to mix a lot of extra formula. Then I poured the measured amount into the leaky feeding bucket. That little calf went for it and while he kept on drinking, I kept pouring in as much — if not more — formula as I saw dripping out from the bottom. The calf got his dinner…as long as I was certain to pour it in faster than it trickled out.

That memory replayed in my mind recently when I heard a pastor talking about being filled with the Spirit. He was describing the despondency of so many Christians he counsels. Believers who find themselves filled with the Spirit one day, and emptied out the next. They're frustrated, and tired of getting drained-and-filled, drained-and-filled.

Those Christians, I reasoned, are simply leaky buckets. Welcome to the club! *All of us* are like leaky buckets, simply because we're human. And this whole cycle of getting drained and then filled up can be tiring if we try and go it alone.

The answer? It's simple. Make sure you've got somebody (or perhaps a great many somebodies) pouring their love and counsel and prayers into you faster than you find it leaking out.

Fellowship. That's the solution. Brothers and sisters who will hold you accountable, study with you, sharpen you, and keep you on the straight path. Imperfect, "leaky" Christians who will pray for you as you pray for them.

Oh sure. Your faith will keep leaking; you'll keep losing the zeal and fervor and excitement as you walk through life. Sorry, but this side of heaven that's inevitable. Just make sure you're part of a fellowship where you'll be filled up faster than you empty out. You might even find your "leaky" bucket overflowing into some of the empty buckets around you.

That's what being in the Body is all about.

Day 18

The Glorious Pursuit

We who are strong ought to bear with the failings
of the weak and not to please ourselves. Each of
us should please his neighbor for his good, to build
him up.

ROMANS 15:1–2

Let us consider how we may spur one another on
toward love and good deeds. Let us not give up
meeting together, as some are in the habit of doing,
but let us encourage one another.

HEBREWS 10:24–25

*"No man is an island." Are you convinced of the truth of John
Donne's famous assertion? It's thoroughly biblical. How many fellow
believers can you lean on in times of need? Even one good Christian
friend can make a huge difference. If you find yourself short in the
fellowship department, ask God for wisdom to find a few trusted
brothers and sisters. Then take a risk. Trust someone enough to tell
them you need their counsel and prayers. You need their fellowship.*

Day 19

DRIFTING

When I was a child, our family always spent summer vacations beach camping near Dewey Beach, Delaware. The crashing waves on that shoreline held no fear for me, and day after day I begged Mother to let me follow my older sisters into the water. Finally giving in to my pleas one beautiful morning, she strapped me tightly into my life vest and sternly warned my sisters to keep hold of my hand. Kathy held me on her hip as we waded through the breakers into the rolling surf. It was quieter there behind the thundering waves, and I giggled and laughed with Kathy and Jay as we rode the rollercoaster swells.

Somehow, at some point, I let go of Kathy's hand. And after the next great swell, it suddenly occurred to me that my sisters were nowhere near. When I saw their heads pop up over another swell, I realized with horror how far I had been carried away.

I was adrift in the wide ocean—and going farther from shore.

I don't know how it happened…and so quickly! A strong current had caught me, pulling me down the beach. Thankfully, at that moment my mother ran from her umbrella, dove into the sea, and rescued me.

I never realized how far I had drifted until the moment I saw that great distance between me and the others.

As the writer of Hebrews affirms, none of us can afford to drift. "We must pay more careful attention, therefore, to what we have heard, so that we do not drift away" (Hebrews 2:1).

Drifting can be dangerous. Always, always, currents are pulling at us. Always we are swimming upstream, against the tide. There is always the temptation to drift, and we never realize how far we are carried away until we see Christ—and until we see the others from whom we've parted.

It's possible for *any* of us to drift spiritually or morally. No one is immune. Think of the powerful currents in your own life that can take hold and carry you along unless you make an effort to control the direction. There is the current of social opinion, of fashion or fad. There is a current of personal desire…doing the things *you* want to do. Lust is a powerful undertow. Materialism is a relentless tug.

I'm very aware of such currents in my own life. The Bible calls it walking "according to the course of this world" (Ephesians 2:2, NASB). But as I look back over my activities and opportunities of recent years, I realize I must continue to pull on the oars with all the strength God gives me.

Because, you see, I'm one of those people who could easily drift, giving myself to whatever current is bearing me along. In order to keep my life from aimlessly coasting, I must make every effort to keep my focus on Jesus. I've got to pull myself in line with God's Word every morning as I begin my day. I need to constantly aim and re-aim my life in a God-honoring direction. I've got to tug at my heart to keep it from wandering off into daydreams or silly temptations.

Following God doesn't come easy for me. It probably never will. But year after year, I recommit to keep at the oars, rowing against those strong currents. With God's help, next year I will look back on another 365 days of hard-fought, hard-won progress in my walk with Christ.

Let's put our shoulders to those oars together, shall we?

The Glorious Pursuit

We demolish arguments and every pretension that sets itself up against the knowledge of God, and we take captive every thought to make it obedient to Christ.

2 CORINTHIANS 10:5

Then we will no longer be infants, tossed back and
forth by the waves, and blown here and there by
every wind of teaching and by the cunning and
craftiness of men in their deceitful scheming.

Ephesians 4:14

*A passionate faith cannot afford to let down its guard against
the world's pull or against our own sinful desires. Passivity and
passion are mutually exclusive. Ask God now for the strength and
spiritual alertness to actively resist these strong currents. And trust
Him to keep you refreshed, so that with every battle you win, you
will grow stronger in Him.*

DAY 20

OPEN MY EYES

ent on destroying the prophet Elisha, the king of Syria received reliable information that the man he sought was living in the walled city of Dothan.

The king wasn't taking any chances. Rather than sending a couple of hit men to liquidate Elisha, the king mobilized "horses and chariots and a strong force" (2 Kings 6:14). The massive Syrian force came by night and surrounded the city, readying for an early-morning assault.

At daybreak, Elisha's servant went out for a casual morning stroll along the top of the wall, pausing to fill his eyes with the tranquil sunrise over the surrounding hills. What he saw must have made the blood freeze in his veins. The morning sun gleamed and flashed from count-less shields, helmets, chariot wheels, arrows, and spear tips. A thousand colorful banners fluttered in the soft breeze.

Filled with sheer terror and dismay, the attendant scampered back to the prophet's chamber with the tid-ings of gloom and doom. "Oh, my lord, what shall we do?" (v. 15).

If the servant was expecting his master to fly into a panic or tear out what remained of his sparse hair, he was in for a surprise. He was probably even more surprised by Elisha's calm reply: "Don't be afraid…. Those who are with us are more than those who are with them" (v. 16).

Elisha was not afraid of the Syrian king and his intimi-dating army. For he trusted in One who could not be seen with the physical eye.

But Elisha did more than give a devotional homily to

his frightened servant. He prayed for him, saying, "O LORD, open his eyes so he may see." The Lord answered and the servant "looked and saw the hills full of horses and chariots of fire all around Elisha" (v. 17).

I like that story. Because when we're serving the Lord, fighting off temptation, or making a stand against fear, we may tend to feel lonely on our side of the battle lines. The devil has his troops marshaled against us, and we are too easily overcome with discouragement or fright. After all, look at what we're up against! Bastions of secularism. Strong political lobbies. Pornography running rampant. Racism. Injustice. Stumbling Christian leaders.

At such a time when fear grips your heart and your faith weakens and wavers, pray that the Lord will open your eyes…that you may see.

There's no less of a force surrounding you on the front lines of the battlefield than there was in Elisha's day. A host of angels? A legion of saints? A mountain of horses and chariots of fire? Probably. But all you really need is the One who promised never to leave or forsake you—the One who said, "Surely I am with you always" (Matthew 28:20).

You don't need an army on your side when you've got the King of kings.

The Glorious Pursuit

I keep asking that the God of our Lord Jesus Christ, the glorious Father, may give you the Spirit of wisdom and revelation, so that you may know him better. I pray also that the eyes of your heart may be enlightened in order that you may know the hope to which he has called you, the riches of his glorious inheritance in the saints, and his incomparably great power for us who believe.

EPHESIANS 1:17–19

Take your worst fear, your most imposing enemy. Set it up beside the God of the Bible. See how small it really is? Now realize that even that helpful perspective probably "sees" the problem larger than it is and God smaller than He truly is. Ask Him to keep enlarging your vision of Him. And ask for the faith to believe that He's still greater than you could ever imagine.

Day 21

THE FIRST LINE
OF DEFENSE

By all rights it was a battle God's people should
never have won.

The odds against King Jehoshaphat and his outnum-
bered troops were astronomical. Several neighboring
military powers had banded together, determined to wipe
the little nation of Judah off the map (see 2 Chronicles 20).

By the time Jehoshaphat got the bad news—"a vast
army is coming against you from Edom, from the other

side of the Sea" (v. 2) — there was very little he could do
about it. The awesome force was less than thirty miles
from Jerusalem's gates.

The frightened king took stock of what he had on
hand. It wasn't much. He had no strategy, no chariots, no
defense, no allies, no time, and no army worth writing
home about.

But whether he knew it or not, he did have a secret
weapon.

> Alarmed, Jehoshaphat resolved to inquire of the
> LORD, and he proclaimed a fast for all Judah. The
> people of Judah came together to seek help from
> the LORD; indeed, they came from every town in
> Judah to seek him.... All the men of Judah, with
> their wives and children and little ones, stood
> there before the LORD.
>
> VV. 3–4, 13

The king poured his heart out before God and all the
people. He didn't bluff or bluster. He didn't rattle his

saber or make a patriotic speech. He just prayed as though his life depended on it—and it did.

> O LORD, God of our fathers, are you not the God who is in heaven? You rule over all the kingdoms of the nations. Power and might are in your hand, and no one can withstand you.... We have no power to face this vast army that is attacking us. We do not know what to do, but our eyes are upon you.
>
> VV. 6, 12

The enemy was a determined marching multitude, but Jehoshaphat's only armor was his faith in a prophet's message.

> This is what the LORD says to you: "Do not be afraid or discouraged because of this vast army. For the battle is not yours, but God's.... You will not have to fight this battle. Take up your positions; stand firm and see the deliverance the LORD will give you."
>
> VV. 15, 17

This was to be no usual battle. So the king didn't even pretend to follow accepted military procedure.

> After consultation with the leaders of the people, [the king] determined that there should be a choir leading the march, clothed in sanctified garments and singing the song "His Loving-Kindness Is Forever" as they walked along praising and thanking the LORD!
>
> V. 21, TLB

Talk about your out-of-the-ordinary weapon of warfare! Who ever heard of putting a choir out in front of an army? Harps and lyres leading the infantry instead of tanks and artillery? How could such a thing work? And yet work it did.

> At the moment they began to sing and to praise, the Lord caused the armies of Ammon, Moab, and Mount Seir to begin fighting among themselves, and they destroyed each other!… When the army

of Judah arrived at the watchtower that looks out
over the wilderness, as far as they could look there
were dead bodies lying on the ground—not a
single one of the enemy had escaped.

VV. 22, 24, TLB

Now, that marvelous story is more than just a histori-
cal event. It has meaning for you and me this very day.
Like Jehoshaphat, we are surrounded by multitudes of
enemies.

Well trained and well equipped, the armies of Satan
are experts at battling believers. And what one of us, in
our own strength and with our meager personal resources,
can withstand all those fiery darts?

How do we face such an overpowering enemy?

Ask Jehoshaphat. He would tell you that the answer
is *praise to the Lord*. The demons hate it. Human opponents
are irritated by it. But you and I need to learn to praise
God in such a way that our enemy will be thrown into a
complete rout. When we step out into spiritual warfare
(which, by the way, happens every day), we have the

resources in Christ to totally confuse our foe.

We do it with our praise.

This is such a difficult lesson for me to learn. When things go haywire in my life, it's my second nature to *do* something—anything—to remedy, rectify, or resolve the problem. Make lists…set goals…get counseling…go shopping…raid the fridge…read a book on the subject…talk it out with others. Keeping busy seems like such a logical frontline defense against the devil's attacks.

But praise? What good can talking into thin air do? How is it that words pack enough power to thwart a determined adversary? Won't my enemies—discouragement and despondency—be better defeated by rolling up my sleeves, making fists, and meeting them head-on?

Yet we learn from Jehoshaphat that praise must be our *first* line of defense.

Paul put it in a nutshell for the Corinthians: "For though we live in the world, we do not wage war as the world does. The weapons we fight with are not the weapons of the world" (2 Corinthians 10:3–4).

All those legions lined up against us will turn on one another when they hear us lifting high the name of our mighty Lord Jesus.

You've got power over the enemy. Right now. It's praise.

The Glorious Pursuit

Sing praises to God, sing praises; sing praises to our King, sing praises. For God is the King of all the earth; sing to him a psalm of praise.

PSALM 47:6–7

Confront your Enemy. Praise God about His character and His amazing deeds. Flip to Psalm 105 and recite it out loud to Him. Think of every good gift, every happy moment, every breathtaking experience of delight and wonder... Now thank God for all these things and recount them to anyone else who will listen. Then watch Him add yet another amazing deed to the long, long list.

WHAT YOU CAN AND CAN'T CONTROL

*I*t's one thing to reflect a submissive attitude toward God when we bring troubles on ourselves, but it's a different matter when unexpected trials smash us broadside—trials not of our own making.

A drunk driver veers across the yellow line. A grim-faced doctor diagnoses some strange cancer. Reassessment slaps your property into a higher tax bracket. Some dumb linebacker breaks your high schooler's leg in football practice. A quick-handed thief lifts your purse or wallet. An old friend drags your name through the mud.

These are circumstances, allowed by God, over which you have no control. And they're the hardest ones to deal with.

But let's look for a moment at the apostle Paul. Talk about getting blindsided with problems for which he had no responsibility! Listen, Paul didn't bring that shipwreck on himself. It wasn't his idea to generate a death threat in Damascus and face the humiliation of leaving town in a basket lowered over the wall. It was never in his mind to orchestrate a mob scene in Lystra, leaving him smashed by stones and left for dead. Was it his choice to enlist a shrill-voiced slave girl to follow him around, causing a ruckus that gave him a bad name? And when he answered people's questions, could he help it if they were outraged by the truth?

No, Paul may not have been responsible for his circumstances. But Paul was responsible for the way he *responded* to those circumstances.

And how did he respond? He didn't groan, "Oh, for

Pete's sake, here we go again." Instead, he said, "For Christ's sake, I delight in weaknesses.... For when I am weak, then I am strong" (2 Corinthians 12:10). He said, "Therefore I endure everything for the sake of the elect, that they too may obtain the salvation that is in Christ Jesus, with eternal glory" (2 Timothy 2:10).

Consider the incident in Philippi, described in Acts 16. The magistrates handcuffed Paul and Silas to a scourging pole and gave them a brutal whipping. Piling humiliation upon humiliation, the Philippian authorities then took the bruised and lacerated missionaries and placed them in stocks in an inner cell of the city jail. There they were, stuck in a wet, stinky dungeon tucked far away from the light of day.

Paul must have been faint. Silas must have been sick to his stomach. Every bone ached and their fresh wounds oozed.

Yet, deep in the dark dungeon, they did something incredible. At midnight, the darkest and loneliest hour, they began praying and singing praises to God. They weren't just humming along lightly or mumbling their prayers in between moans and groans. No, Luke says that in spite of the thick walls and heavy doors, the other prisoners "were listening to them" (v. 25).

Their words won the battle against Satan in that midnight hour. A passionate faith is unstoppable.

As it says in Psalm 106:47, "Save us, O LORD our God, and gather us…that we may give thanks to your holy name *and glory in your praise*" (emphasis mine). To whine or grumble, fret or murmur, complain or lament would have been to invite defeat in that terrible hour. And who would have blamed Paul and Silas if they had sputtered a nasty remark or two?

But the record shows they didn't. They didn't succumb to defeat with thoughtless, ill-tempered words. They triumphed in a victory of praise. What a witness to the other prisoners! What a testimony to the jailer! And what an encouragement to countless generations of oppressed believers who have read that account and found fresh courage.

Words. Do we fully understand their power? Can any of us really grasp the mighty force behind the things we say? Do we stop and think before we speak, considering the potency of the phrases we utter?

No wonder the Bible gives so much attention to the phrases that pass through our lips. Little wonder the book of James gives the tongue such a vigorous once-over. How can we bless at one moment and curse at another? How can sweet water and bitter bubble up from the same spring? I shudder to think of all the times during the course of one day that I mutter a complaint or manipulate with a precisely timed phrase or two.

If you and I are looking for victory over our circumstances, we will find it in praise. No matter how much your kids bug you, no matter how often you feel stepped on by others, no matter what the circumstances at home or the office…success is possible when we hold our spiteful tongue and win the battle with words that bless our Lord.

We *are* responsible. Maybe we're not accountable for some of our trials, but we are accountable for all of our responses.

If Paul and Silas could sing choruses in a dungeon, you can offer praise wherever life places you—this very moment!

The Glorious Pursuit

Why are you downcast, O my soul? Why so disturbed within me? Put your hope in God, for I will yet praise him, my Savior and my God.

PSALM 42:11

Sometimes praise escapes from our lips spontaneously. We can't hold it in. At other times it's a choice, a sheer act of will. But in both situations, meaningful praise is just as precious to God. And He responds just as powerfully in both cases, not necessarily as we expect, but always to our greatest good and His greatest glory. Take a minute to pay Him the highest compliment now, maybe in song, maybe in speech, or maybe in the silence of your soul.

WHEN GOD CONCEALS

*I*t is the glory of God to conceal a matter" (Proverbs 25:2). Goes against the grain a little, doesn't it?

We don't want matters concealed from us. Especially things that touch our lives. We want all the facts, the blueprint of God's design spread out on the table.

It is the glory of God to conceal a matter.

Consider the life of Amy Carmichael. She went to India in 1895, not realizing that country would become her home, the children of India her family. Nor did she know then that many beautiful, intelligent little girls in India were being taken from their homes and trained to become temple women to satisfy the lusts of men in the worship of Hindu gods. She learned of this horrible custom when a seven-year-old who had escaped from a temple was brought to her house.

From that day on the Lord placed the desire in Amy Carmichael's heart to save these girls from moral ruin and train them to do the will of their heavenly Father.

Yet after over three decades of ministry, Miss Carmichael slipped into a pit, permanently crippling her leg. For the next *twenty years* she remained in bed, rarely leaving her room.

On the morning of the accident she had prayed, "Do anything, Lord, that will fit me to serve You better."

That accident was the answer. But in her confinement she went on to write thirteen books which have blessed generations of sufferers around the world.

It is the glory of God to conceal a matter.

"We speak of God's secret wisdom," Paul writes, "a wisdom that has been hidden and that God destined for our glory before time began" (1 Corinthians 2:7).

It is a glorious thing for a man or woman to be God-sufficient and not seek human explanations for His actions in his or her life. Even when those circumstances are totally mysterious. As in the case of Amy Carmichael, the glory of the believer is absolute trust and confidence.

It is a glorious thing to know that your Father God makes no mistakes in directing or permitting that which crosses the path of your life.

It is the glory of God to conceal a matter.

It is *our* glory to trust Him, no matter what.

The Glorious Pursuit

The secret things belong to the LORD our God, but the things revealed belong to us and to our children forever, that we may follow all the words of this law.

DEUTERONOMY 29:29

Now faith is being sure of what we hope for and certain of what we do not see.

HEBREWS 11:1

A passionate faith trusts in the Person, and can therefore move ahead when the future is unknown. Ask God for insight about your future, but ask even more fervently for a deeper personal knowledge of Him. He may not say yes to the first, but His answer is always affirmative to the second.

PILGRIM OR TOURIST?

When I was growing up, we used to visit my Uncle Ted's ranch in Tie Siding, Wyoming.

What an adventure! It was a real working cattle ranch with plenty of chores for young Maryland cowgirls. My sisters and I even had a part in branding some of the calves.

Uncle Ted put me on a big old retired workhorse. It was my job to keep the cows corralled at one end of the arena while at the other end the cowboys would use their cutting horses to single out calves for branding. Even though my horse and I just stood there most of the time, watching all the action across the way, I still felt as though I had a special job minding those cows.

Because my Uncle Ted's ranch was situated near Laramie, tourists would often come by to take a look at what a real cattle ranch was all about. They would stand at a polite distance, casually observing all the goings-on, occasionally pointing, or pulling out their cameras.

I was just a little tyke then, but I can remember straightening my cowboy hat and sitting up in my saddle to pose for snapshots—as though I were a permanent fixture around the place. It never occurred to me back then that I was just passing through like those tourists—that I was only going to be at the ranch a short time.

Yet even though Uncle Ted's was not my permanent place of residence, I got a lot more involved than the average tourist. For a short time at least, I was part of a working ranch.

It's been years since I've visited Tie Siding. But to this day I've resisted the label of "tourist." Whenever I visit places around the world, I'm not satisfied to stand at a distance snapping pictures. I like to get involved. To do things. To talk with people who live in the area. To learn about customs. I don't want to be considered a tourist with funny clothes and a Kodak. I want to be part of things.

As a Christian living out the kingdom of God down here on earth, I feel the same way. True, the Bible tells us we are to be pilgrims on this planet. That is, we must not mistake this world for home.

But I don't think Scripture encourages us to be mere "tourists" either—casually observing all the goings-on around us at a polite, safe distance. "You are the salt of the earth," Jesus told us in Matthew 5:13. "You are the light of the world" (v. 14). God wants us to get involved, to rub shoulders with folks around us, even though we're only going to be here for a season. We've got work to do here—and only a short time to do it.

Do you consider yourself a pilgrim when it comes to living out the life of Christ? Or are you more like a tourist, staying arm's length from any kind of serious involvement in your church, neighborhood, and community?

There are too many tourists crowding their way through life already. God doesn't want any more spectators. He needs pilgrims, sober-minded and serious, who will make their impact for Him on their way through this life and into the next.

So put your camera away and climb on a horse, pardner. There's room in the corral for you.

The Glorious Pursuit

Dear friends, I urge you, as aliens and strangers in the world, to abstain from sinful desires, which war against your soul. Live such good lives among the pagans that, though they accuse you of doing wrong, they may see your good deeds and glorify God on the day he visits us.

1 PETER 2:11–12

[Jesus] looked toward heaven and prayed,
"Father.... As you sent me into the world, I have
sent them into the world."

John 17:1, 18

God calls us to hold tightly to His hand, and with that firm grasp to throw ourselves into loving ministry to others. He loves to intrude into the lives of hurting, needy people around us…through our kind words and actions. He also loves to see us sharpen one another as we nudge each other closer toward holy living. What opportunities has He laid before you?

Day 25

WHO HELPS THE MOST?

People will often ask me, "Who helped you the most when you were hurting?"

That's a good question, but I can never seem to come up with a fast answer. I guess that's because there was no one person—no famous writer, no brainy seminary student, no super-sensitive counselor.

No, answers to my questions didn't come from "extraordinary" people. Frankly, when I was first injured in my diving accident and left paralyzed, I wasn't *looking* for wisdom or knowledge.

At first I was just looking for love.

You don't have to have a PhD or a master's from some Bible college in order to give love. Average, commonplace people are just as necessary in the healing process as counselors and theologians. All of us have the capacity to give love to someone who is hurting.

That should be good news to you—especially those of you looking for ways to alleviate the pain of a friend in the hospital or a family member going through a crushing disappointment. If you and I are truly looking for an answer to the question, *How do I help those who are in pain?* we don't have to have a lot of answers. We don't even have to know all the specialized Scriptures or 101 reasons God allows suffering. All we've got to know is love.

The only Scripture we might need at first is 1 Corinthians 13. We don't have to understand whether people in pain want to be cheered up or consoled. We don't have to rationalize, wondering, *What possible good could* my *presence do?* We don't have to guess whether somebody wants to talk about his suffering or not. Instead of getting yourself all tangled up in those guessing games, remember: The only thing you really need to give is love.

I most appreciated those people who came into the hospital armed with love—and *Seventeen* magazines and Winchell's doughnuts. I appreciated friends dropping by to help me write letters or bringing writing paper and envelopes—even stamps. I was super impressed when others bought birthday cards for me to send to a friend whose special day was coming up. I especially remember a few girls who made it a weekly ritual to come by and do my nails. What fun!

These were people who helped. They weren't trained counselors. They weren't spiritual giants. They weren't biblical wizards. They weren't PhDs. They weren't even full of all kinds of knowledge and wisdom. They were just commonplace, everyday sorts of people who gave me what I needed most of all: God's love in action.

The Glorious Pursuit

Jesus replied: "'Love the Lord your God with all your heart and with all your soul and with all your

mind.' This is the first and greatest commandment.
And the second is like it: 'Love your neighbor as
yourself.'"

MATTHEW 22:37–39

Love never fails.

1 CORINTHIANS 13:8

*A passionate faith is a compassionate faith. It takes action on
behalf of others in any way it can. What's some simple way you
can touch a life, even if just by your presence or your caring, listening ear?*

Day 26

DON'T TOUCH THE TAR BABY

Do you remember the Uncle Remus story of Brer Rabbit and the tar baby?

I can close my eyes and see old tar baby sitting on a log near the dear old brier patch and Brer Rabbit's front door. Someone had plunked a hat on his head, stuck a pipe in his mouth, and there tar baby sat, waiting for an unsuspecting passerby to come along and give his hand a shake. (I suspect Brer Fox laying a trap for Brer Rabbit.)

And then that poor somebody would be hopelessly stuck to that sticky, icky black tar. Everybody, if they knew what was good for them, should have avoided that tar baby.

I once read an article in which the author gave fresh meaning to that old story. He asked, do you know any tar babies—people better avoided, loaded down with problems? Folks you'd rather not approach or come near?

Are there any tar babies in your church? I keep thinking of a pretty tar baby named Carol.

Carol and her family are members at a prominent evangelical church. She is an outstanding senior at a Christian high school. Everyone was stunned to hear that she had become pregnant. Her school refused to let her continue her education. The whole family is hurting as I write these words, in desperate need of somebody who will just mingle some tears with their tears—even in their disgrace.

But the church stands awkwardly by, shuffling its feet, not knowing how to mix reproof and correction with love and encouragement.

Is it possible that we're so anxious to protect our spiritual reputation—or the reputation of our church—that we deliberately avoid the "contamination" of helping people in deep spiritual trouble?

Do we think they will somehow tempt us to sin, too?

Do we suppose that an "example" should be made of a wrong done?

Do we fear that our loyalty to somebody in trouble tars us with their disgrace?

No, we certainly do not need a casual attitude toward sin. And yes, we should deal with wrongdoing in a straightforward way. But we need to couple that direct approach with love and comfort for those who are broken apart by the shame and humiliation of a sin.

People in trouble should not be viewed as tar babies, waiting to glue others into the sticky mess they've made of themselves.

Paul had a better idea. He wrote to the church at Galatia:

Even if a man should be detected in some sin, my brothers, the spiritual ones among you should

quietly set him back on the right path, not with
any feeling of superiority but being yourselves on
guard against temptation. Carry each other's bur-
dens and so live out the law of Christ. If a man
thinks he is "somebody" when he is nobody, he is
deceiving himself.

Galatians 6:1–3, Phillips

Paul is saying that hurting, stumbling people are not
tar babies. To deliberately look the other way and give
them a wide berth is not "discipline." It is spiritual snob-
bery—and a direct affront to the law of Christ.

Has someone come to your mind as you've read these
words? Can you visualize his face, feel his shame and
hurt? Take the apostle's advice. Restore that person...qui-
etly, gently. Today. Mingle your tears with his. Touch his
disgrace. Just as Jesus touched yours.

God forbid, but there may come a day when the tar
baby's shoe is on the other foot.

Day 26

The Glorious Pursuit

What do you think? If a man owns a hundred
sheep, and one of them wanders away, will he not
leave the ninety-nine on the hills and go to look for
the one that wandered off? And if he finds it, I tell
you the truth, he is happier about that one sheep
than about the ninety-nine that did not wander
off.... If your brother sins against you, go and
show him his fault, just between the two of you. If
he listens to you, you have won your brother over.

MATTHEW 18:12–13, 15

*It's easy to pray with compassion and empathy for those we
love or respect. It's harder to pray for the societal outcasts — a
neighbor with AIDS, a church member who's schizophrenic, or a
homosexual struggling to change his lifestyle. Does someone come
to mind? Even if you don't feel compassionate toward him or her,
you can show compassion, first by praying. Take a few minutes
now to show love toward someone who may be one of the loneliest
people you know.*

Day 27

DYING OF THIRST

*J*ohann is young, tall, blond, and Dutch. I got to know him through my cousin, who attended the same Bible school in England. Gifted and handsome, Johann could have carved out a comfortable youth ministry in his native Netherlands—or most anywhere in the world, for that matter.

Comfort, however, isn't one of Johann's major goals. He chose to take the gospel of Christ to the bedouins and nomads near Israel's barren Sinai desert. A forgotten people in one of the most desolate corners of the world.

Johann works by an oasis near the sea, attracting travelers and bedouins by offering hot meals, clothing, and first aid. Following this hospitality, he tells Bible stories and gives a simple testimony of his faith in the One who walked the same sandy waste, two thousand years ago.

The work isn't easy. Loneliness stalks those sun-scorched regions. Bibles and other supplies are few and far between. But Johann's desire to proclaim Christ is greater than all these obstacles. He has a message to offer—and considers it every bit as valuable as the life-giving water he ladles out to his guests.

From the bedouins, Johann learned it is considered worse than murder if you know of a water source and yet neglect to tell your fellow man.

Few of us will ever live in a wilderness like the one where young Johann has pitched his tent. Not many among us will ever proclaim salvation to desert nomads. But all around us, no matter where we reside or work, there are thirsty men and women. The neighbor down the street, the man at the service station, the boy who carries our groceries, the secretary who types and files, or even the distant aunt who occasionally comes by for visits.

If these people don't know Christ, they're going to die of thirst.

In John 4, Jesus had a conversation with a thirsty woman. It was a hot, dry day in a town near the edge of the desert. Sitting on the edge of an ancient well, He talked to the woman about two kinds of thirst: the immediate physical sort, and a deeper, more profound thirst of the soul.

"Everyone who drinks of this water will thirst again," He told her, "but whoever drinks of the water that I will give him shall never thirst; but the water that I will give him will become in him a well of water springing up to eternal life" (vv. 13–14, NASB).

The woman left her water pot unfilled and hurried back into the city. Yet her thirst was quenched that day as never before. She had found a deeper well than the one in the village square. She had found the Source of living water and didn't waste a moment before telling everyone in town.

Do you know the Source of living water? If you do, please don't withhold a drink from somebody who is thirsty.

It's not just a matter of hospitality. It's a matter of life and death.

The Glorious Pursuit

Then the angel showed me the river of the water of life, as clear as crystal, flowing from the throne of God and of the Lamb down the middle of the great street of the city. On each side of the river stood the tree of life…. Whoever is thirsty, let him come; and whoever wishes, let him take the free gift of the water of life.

REVELATION 22:1–2, 17

It's easier for us to share life with others when we realize that, inwardly, they're more passionate in their thirst than we often are to help them satisfy it. Many dying people hide their thirst; look past their apparent contentment and see the desperation inside.

Then show them the way to the Source of Life. Sometimes we allow embarrassment, awkwardness, or a loss of urgency to weaken our witness of Christ. Think of your neighbors or relatives who do not know Jesus in a personal way—these people are dehydrated spiritually. Share your heart for your Savior with them…it'll be a refreshing drink for their weary souls.

Day 28

LET YOUR LIFE
OVERFLOW

I was reading Psalm 23 the other day and pulled to a dead stop at three familiar words: *"My cup overflows"* (v. 5).

What in the world does that mean?

When something overflows, we usually think of *waste*. Water that overflows a dam rushes out to sea. Gas that overflows a tank pollutes the ground. Coffee that overflows a cup stains the carpet. Milk that overflows a measuring cup drains down the sink. Most folks tend to equate overflow with squandered resources.

But what about a *life* that overflows? What about a man or woman who brims over with the joy and grace and love of God? Is it all down the drain? Listen to how Romans 15:13 describes it: "May the God of hope fill you with all joy and peace as you trust in him, so that you may overflow with hope by the power of the Holy Spirit."

God must think that sort of overflow is a good idea. He doesn't seem a bit worried about a wasted resource.

Paul might have put his finger on a reason for that in his letter to the Thessalonians: "May the Lord make your love increase and overflow for each other and for everyone else, just as ours does for you" (1 Thessalonians 3:12).

What a picture! God doesn't intend your life to overflow down the storm drain or evaporate into the air. He wants it to soak others! The spillover of His love and goodness in our lives is to benefit and encourage those around us.

You can't escape it. It's unavoidable. If you want to make an impact for Christ on your family, friends, neighbors, or coworkers, then let God fill you with His joy and peace as you trust Him—just like it says in Romans. He'll fill that cup of yours to the brim, and then pour in more. And over it goes, right over the edges of your soul. Your love will stream out in all directions.

Your joy will cascade like an artesian well, soaking into the thirsty ground of the discouraged and cynical lives around you.

"It was by the generosity of God…that the love of God overflowed for the benefit of all men," Paul wrote in Romans. God wants *you* to benefit others, too. So let your cup run over. It's no waste. Nothing will go down the drain or be lost. Trust Him. Obey Him. Then let God open His floodgates in your life, pouring in more of His grace and peace than you could possibly contain.

Listen, you conservative Christians…God has never asked any of us to conserve His love.

The Glorious Pursuit

Dear friends, since God so loved us, we also ought to love one another.

1 JOHN 4:11

Freely you have received, freely give.

MATTHEW 10:8

God's grace should be contagious. You've caught it. Give it to someone else. There are hundreds of ways you can spill over into the lives of others. Seek God's guidance about the ways that are best suited to you and the people around you. Then let them drink from His grace pouring through you.

Day 29

KEEPING IN STEP

Since we live by the Spirit, let us keep in step with the Spirit" (Galatians 5:25). That's good advice for those of us who try to live too far ahead in the future.

We book our calendars through June before the first March daffodils poke through the frost. Our minds range far and wide over distant, misty horizons and our eyes strain to peer over hills and around corners. When obstacles loom in the path of our carefully plotted course, we think of them as "barriers" to our goals and objectives.

In a society where we're pushed forward so quickly, we tend to forget it's the *moment* that counts.

That's why I love verses like Galatians 5:25. How in the world can we expect to live by the Spirit if we seek to move through life mile by mile rather than step by step? Our walk in the Spirit is to be just that—a walk, not a sprint.

When we get ahead of ourselves, we end up disregarding the present...the people around us right now...the opportunities immediately at hand.

When we get ahead of ourselves, we make the mistake of ignoring the specifics. Specifics like sin. And instant obedience. Preoccupied with future agendas, we don't have the energy to engage in that daily, moment-by-moment struggle with the sinful, selfish habits that dog our feet.

When we're keeping in step with the Spirit, He can pinpoint those areas in our lives that need change. But when we get ahead of Him, trying to take life in leaps rather than steps, we tend to gloss over the daily obstacles and challenges.

Our prayers become too general.

Our Bible reading becomes merely a 10K run that needs to get finished.

Our obedience centers around a lot of outward actions rather than a daily cleansing.

Jesus becomes a "goal" rather than a Person to whom we relate moment by moment.

Heaven gets placed on a shelf in the faraway future rather than on a meal table marked "today."

So what I say to you, I say to myself. *Slow down.* Take time to chew on a few meaty words from James the apostle…and Jesus the Lord:

> Now listen, you who say, "Today or tomorrow we
> will go to this or that city, spend a year there,
> carry on business and make money." Why, you do
> not even know what will happen tomorrow. What

is your life? You are a mist that appears for a little while and then vanishes. Instead, you ought to say, "If it is the Lord's will, we will live and do this or that." As it is, you boast and brag. All such boasting is evil.

James 4:13–16

Seek first his kingdom and his righteousness, and all these things will be given to you as well. Therefore do not worry about tomorrow, for tomorrow will worry about itself. Each day has enough trouble of its own.

Matthew 6:33–34

The Christian faith is meant to be lived moment by moment. It isn't some broad, general outline—it's a long walk with a real Person. Details count: passing thoughts, small sacrifices, a few encouraging words, little acts of kindness, brief victories over nagging sins.

If you're going to walk with Me, the Spirit seems to be saying, *pay attention to the present.*

If you keep running ahead, you may find yourself walking solo. And that's not only dangerous, it's lonely.

The Glorious Pursuit

Do not be anxious about anything, but in everything, by prayer and petition, with thanksgiving, present your requests to God. And the peace of God, which transcends all understanding, will guard your hearts and your minds in Christ Jesus.

PHILIPPIANS 4:6–7

I pray that out of his glorious riches he may strengthen you with power through his Spirit in your inner being, so that Christ may dwell in your hearts through faith.

EPHESIANS 3:16–17

Every moment of every day, Jesus is walking beside you. His Holy Spirit is living inside you. That's reality. But—amazingly, sadly—we forget about Him. Growing toward a passionate faith means, in part, learning to more consistently enjoy the immense privilege of the presence of the Lord of the universe, Jesus Christ, dwelling within you. Bow in your heart to Him now. Talk to Him. He's still there, urging you to keep in step with Him every day.

WHEN GOD OPENS
THE SHUTTERS

*I*f our happiest moments on earth give us a foretaste of heaven, then the tragic moments make us long for it.

The truth of the matter is, I never used to think much about heaven when I was on my feet. It seemed like some vague, distant, misty place where there would be a lot of clouds and harps and we'd polish gold all day—forever! That prospect seemed very unattractive to me—and immensely boring.

Besides, in order to get to heaven, you had to *die*. And at the age of seventeen, who wants to think about that?

But heaven is so wonderful, and it's just like God to give us a little help to turn our thoughts toward that future reality. And sometimes it takes more than a lovely starlit night or a verse of Scripture to open our eyes.

Samuel Rutherford describes this help in an essay he wrote back in the seventeenth century: "If God had told me some time ago that He was about to make me as happy as I could be in this world and then had told me that He should begin by crippling me in arm or limb and removing from me all my usual sources of enjoyment, I should have thought it a very strange mode of accomplishing His purpose. And yet, how is His wisdom manifest even in this. For if you should see a man shut up in a closed room idolizing a set of lamps and rejoicing in their light and you wished to make him truly happy, you would begin by blowing out all of his lamps and then throw open the shutters to let in the light of heaven."

That's just what God did for me when He sent a broken neck my way. He blew out all the lamps in my life which lit up the here and now and made it so exciting. To be sure, the dark depression that followed wasn't much fun. But it certainly made the prospect of heaven come to life. My heart leaps to think of the day when I'll have my new body—hands that feel, arms that hold, and legs that run.

One day God will throw open the shutters. The view that fills our eyes in that moment will make us forget all about the lamps in our shuttered room.

Do you find yourself all caught up in the here and now? Do you sometimes feel like a slave to the clock? Are you sick and tired of struggling with sin or apathy or the anxieties and sorrows that weigh down your heart? God may be using those very things to turn your thoughts toward your future home…and the One who awaits the sound of your steps at the front door.

The Glorious Pursuit

Then I saw a new heaven and a new earth, for the first heaven and the first earth had passed away, and there was no longer any sea. I saw the Holy City, the new Jerusalem, coming down out of heaven from God, prepared as a bride beautifully dressed for her husband. And I heard a loud voice from the throne saying, "Now the dwelling of God is with men, and he will live with them. They will be his people, and God himself will be with them and be their God. He will wipe every tear from their eyes. There will be no more death or mourning or crying or pain, for the old order of things has passed away." He who was seated on the throne said, "I am making everything new!"

REVELATION 21:1–5

What more can I say? Enjoy the view!

Day 31

HOPE ON TIPTOE

*G*etting out into nature is serious business for the Tadas.

This is one Maryland flower that begins to wilt if she can't escape the confines of Los Angeles now and then for short forays among God's handiwork.

Yes, my wheelchair limits our excursions, but it doesn't stop us! Ken and I still love to go camping and boating and fishing—or just exploring.

It could be a desert...we don't live too far from the Mojave and always look forward to desert camping in the early spring. You should see the blooms on the cactus and the yucca plants!

Or the mountains. If we want to catch a breath of fresh air, a short drive along the Los Angeles Crest Highway tops the San Gabriel mountains and offers vistas of craggy peaks and Ponderosa pines.

And then there's the ocean. Only twenty minutes from our house. We'll often take a bag lunch on a Saturday afternoon, park on some cliff, and watch the seagulls swirl and swoop along the crest of the breakers. We always return home with spirits revived and refreshed.

Yes, nature is personal to me. And did you know nature even has its own personal verse in Scripture? Romans 8:19 tells us that "the creation waits in eager expectation for the sons of God to be revealed."

J. B. Phillips renders it like this: "The whole creation is on tiptoe to see the wonderful sight of the sons of God coming into their own."

On tiptoe. In some mysterious way, the flowers and plants and animals and seascapes and landscapes wait in eager expectation for a glory yet to be revealed. Paul tells a little more about this anticipation:

> The world of creation cannot as yet see reality, not because it chooses to be blind, but because in God's purpose it has been so limited—yet it has been given hope. And the hope is that in the end the whole of created life will be rescued from the tyranny of change and decay, and have its share in that magnificent liberty which can only belong to the children of God!
>
> ROMANS 8:20–21, PHILLIPS

The creation is groaning and longing for the day when God will release it from its bondage and usher in a new era with Christ as King. Can you hear the sighing in the wind? Can you feel the heavy silence in the mountains? Can you sense the restless longing in the sea? Something's coming...something better.

But consider this: If the creation has an earnest expectation, surely we believers—the sons and daughters of

God—should have nothing less! If the whole inanimate and brute creation is eagerly expecting, earnestly looking forward to the appearing of Jesus and all that means, this same kind of hope should be much more evident in you and me.

How's *your* hope today?

Do you find yourself longing and looking forward to the glorious appearing of the Lord Jesus Christ? We mustn't wait in a dull sort of way with a ho-hum attitude. We must rejoice in our hope. It's that joy that makes us eagerly expect—like a big Saint Bernard straining at his leash. Anticipation means stretching our necks. Yearning. Fervently hoping.

If that's the sort of attitude that nature has about the coming of that great day, you and I can learn a thing or two from the creation around us. Next time you see a ray of sunlight suddenly pierce through a heavy, dark, afternoon sky, think about Romans 8:19.

If nature waits on tiptoe for the coming of Jesus, you and I shouldn't be caught flat-footed!

The Glorious Pursuit

The Lord himself will come down from heaven,
with a loud command, with the voice of the
archangel and with the trumpet call of God, and
the dead in Christ will rise first. After that, we
who are still alive and are left will be caught up
together with them in the clouds to meet the Lord
in the air. And so we will be with the Lord forever.
Therefore encourage each other with these words.

1 THESSALONIANS 4:16–18

Passion longs for that day. Faith believes it will come. Are
both of these living and growing inside you? Do you want heaven?
Are you confident that it's your destiny? If your focus is on Jesus
Christ, then your answer to both is increasingly YES! Because He
is the essence of heaven's joy. And He is the assurance of heaven's
reality for you. He is both the source and the object of your pas-
sionate faith.

Conclusion

PERPETUAL PASSION, ENDURING FAITH

fter this the Lord chose another seventy-two men and sent them out two by two, to go ahead of him to every town and place where he himself was about to go…. The seventy-two men came back in great joy. 'Lord,' they said, 'even the demons obeyed us when we gave them a command in your name!'" (Luke 10:1, 17, TEV).

Talk about a spiritual shot in the arm! They were the

most exciting days any of the disciples could remember. A few months earlier they had been ordinary working guys, punching a time clock, carrying a lunch box, hassling the daily commute. But now…now they had been transformed into ambassadors of the kingdom of God. Spiritual authority oozed from their pores. It was a heady experience, to say the least.

"Lord, You just wouldn't believe it!" they exulted. "Even the demons took off when we spoke in Your name! It was great!"

This discipleship business was suddenly very interesting. They saw answers to their prayers. They saw people come into the kingdom. They preached fearlessly, prayed passionately, and enjoyed a camaraderie they had never known before. It was like being away on a gigantic spiritual weekend retreat. *Everything* went right…even to the point of controlling the work of demons.

Now, understandably, Jesus was thrilled for them and their newfound joy. He responded with genuine enthusiasm to the success of their ministry. Luke 10:21 says that

He was "filled with joy" (TEV). He burst into prayer and thanked His Father, praising Him that these men had tasted life the way it should be lived.

Yet at the same time, without dampening the spirits of His men, the Lord gently brought fresh focus to their gathering.

Jesus answered them, "I saw Satan fall like lightning from heaven. Listen! I have given you authority, so that you can walk on snakes and scorpions and overcome all the power of the Enemy, and nothing will hurt you. But don't be glad because the evil spirits obey you; rather be glad because your names are written in heaven" (Luke 10:18–20, TEV).

Can you identify with those seventy-two excited missionaries? Perhaps you've found yourself in a similar circumstance.

"Wow, what a great retreat that was!" you say to your friends. You've been away for a week of fellowship with a group of exuberant believers. You've sat under the instruction of a first-rate Christian communicator, and you've come home a changed person. I mean, you've got joy! And that joy carries over for days, even weeks. Your prayers are more passionate; you pray more specifically, with more faith. You even share Christ courageously and fearlessly—you're so excited!

Have you had that happen? Can you recall that feeling of spiritual elation? You thought to yourself, "Oh, if only we could have it this way all of the time. If we could only have that speaker join our church. If we could only experience that sort of fellowship and prayer and excitement on a regular basis! Why does it have to end?"

I think the Lord would like to give us the same focus He gave to His disciples on that first joyous day home from their journey. Don't let your joy depend on a lot of spiritual activities, highlights, and emotions. Don't let your passion or your faith hinge on the next celestial lightning bolt or sun-splashed moment of meditation.

God wants our joy to rest on the simple fact that our names are written in heaven. There is no joy like the joy of our salvation! "Restore to me the joy of your salvation" (Psalm 51:12) was the first request David made of God after he got his spiritual act together.

I hope that in the pages of this book I've helped you understand a few of the countless ways to grow toward a passionate faith. They're all good. They're all solid...part of the foundation on which we stand. But underlying them all is that fact that, if Jesus Christ is your Savior and Lord, there is an entry on an actual page of an actual book in the highest heaven with *your name* on it!

That's the bedrock reason for a perpetual passion, for an enduring faith. You've been transferred from the kingdom of darkness to the kingdom of light. And you get to live throughout eternity in intimate communion with the King of everything!

Hang onto the promise of *Him*, and you'll enjoy a lifelong, unwavering, peaceful, ecstatic, safe, risky, *passionate* faith.

The Disability Outreach of Joni Eareckson Tada

When a diving accident in 1967 robbed Joni of the use of her hands and legs, she found herself sequestered in a hospital ward, depressed and discouraged. Friends from her church rallied and offered help and practical assistance. Seeing how these friends made all the difference in her life, Joni gained a vision to help other churches across the country reach out to families like hers.

Now, almost forty years later, Joni Eareckson Tada leads a worldwide team of skilled staff and volunteers through Joni and Friends, a Christian organization committed to accelerating ministry among families affected by disability. We are energized by the words of Jesus: "Go out and find the disabled and bring them in...so that my Father's house might be full" (Luke 14:13, 23).

If you are disabled, or know of a family affected by disability, we invite you to contact us for more information on our programs and outreach services:

The Joni and Friends International Disability Center
P.O. Box 3333
Agoura Hills, CA 91376
www.joniandfriends.org

You want this immediately.

So you must seek Him passionately!

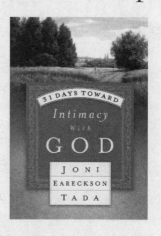

31 Days Toward Intimacy with God

ISBN: 1-59052-002-5

*To know God intimately, trust in Him faithfully,
and depend on Him consistently.*

Journey now along the pathway following the sweet, enticing fragrance of heaven. In every life there are times when the road narrows and the skies grow dark. Seasons of suffering are as certain as the glorious destination before you. Yet you are called to go, and the Source of your spirit's restoration promises to never leave your side.

Daily inspiration from Joni Eareckson Tada gently guides your steps to a closer, more intimate walk with your Savior. And as you travel, new life — His life! — is freely yours as a gift.

Darkness Closes In. The Wind Howls.

You Remain Unshaken.

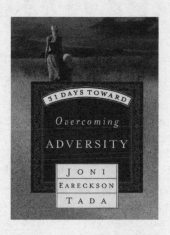

31 Days Toward Overcoming Adversity

ISBN: 1-59052-422-5

When the storm rages and there is no end in sight, how do you survive? Where do you turn, and in whom do you place your trust?

31 Days Toward Overcoming Adversity will guide you not out of the storm, but straight into the eye. Because there in the center is a calm, quiet place where confidence, strength, and even joy can be found.

No stranger to adversity, Joni Eareckson Tada offers daily inspiration that shows you the remarkable in the midst of the impossible. Her thoughtful insights and gentle wisdom will nourish your soul, fill you with hope, and bring you ever closer to the One who never leaves your side.

man in the mirror

For every church to disciple every man

Man in the Mirror believes that Christ has called His church to reach men and help them lead powerful, transformed lives. Since 1986, Man in the Mirror has worked with more than 25,000 churches and millions of men. We help churches reach and disciple men with *three interlocking strategies:*

Leadership Training with No Man Left Behind
Churches that implement the No Man Left Behind Model report a 48% increase in the number of men attending, and an 84% increase in participation in men's discipleship— in just 2 ½ years! We train leaders to cast vision, assess the spiritual state of their men, and develop an intentional plan to disciple all their men. Learn more at maninthemirror.org/ltc

Men's Discipleship with the Journey to Biblical Manhood
The Journey to Biblical Manhood is a flexible process that provides churches with 12 Challenges with fully customizable with templates and timelines to disciple men in the major areas of the Christian life. Learn more at journeytobiblicalmanhood.org

Local Coaching with Area Directors
Area Directors link arms with pastors and leaders in their area to help them disciple men. They serve as local men's discipleship experts to any church that wants help. They also coordinate a local Coalition for Men's Discipleship, made up of churches and leaders committed to the cause. Learn more at areadirectors.org

www.maninthemirror.org

I'm often amazed at how a man will get a hold of a book and how God will use the book to get a hold of the man. —Pat Morley

What are your men and women reading?

Now in boxes of 12 for small groups and giveaways or boxes of 48 for your entire congregation or ministry.

These are just a sampling of the books included in the Books! by the Box program.

Equipped for Life

Finally, a men's devotional magazine for men who are willing to dream big, think big and risk big.

You've never read anything like this. Short devotions written just for men, applying Biblical truth to topics men face every day. Plus, questions to help you go deeper and articles to help you grow and lead others. All in a quarterly magazine that's easy to read and easy to share.

Subscribe today at www.maninthemirror.org

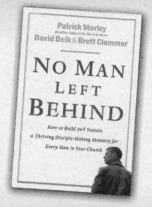